PHOTO BY MEGHAN QUINN

PHOTO BY RICH DEAN

Jennifer Barbee

and **Alex Cohen**

DOWN ⋆ ⋆ ⋆ ⋆ AND DERBY

Jennifer Barbee writes for *Blood & Thunder Magazine* and is a longtime staffer of the Writers Guild of America. **Alex Cohen** is the host of "All Things Considered" on KPCC in Los Angeles and a frequent contributor to National Public Radio. As Kasey Bomber and Axles of Evil, respectively, they have skated with the L.A. Derby Dolls since 2003. They both live in Los Angeles.

DOWN AND

Derby

The Insider's Guide to Roller Derby

Jennifer "Kasey Bomber" Barbee
AND
Alex "Axles of Evil" Cohen

SOFT SKULL PRESS
NEW YORK

For the L.A. Derby Dolls Class of 2003

Library of Congress Cataloging-in-Publication Data

Cohen, Alex
Down and derby : the insider's guide to roller derby / Alex Cohen and Jennifer Barbee.
p. cm.
Includes bibliographical references and index.
ISBN 978-1-59376-274-2 (alk. paper)
1. Roller derbies. 2. Roller skating. I. Barbee, Jennifer. II. Title.
GV859.6.C64 2010
796.21—dc22
2010002725

Cover design by Jay Vollmar
Interior design by Neuwirth & Associates
Printed in the United States of America

Soft Skull Press
An Imprint of Counterpoint LLC
2117 Fourth Street
Suite D
Berkeley, CA 94710

www.softskull.com
www.counterpointpress.com
www.down-and-derby.com

Distributed by Publishers Group West

10 9 8 7 6 5 4 3 2 1

contents

INTRODUCTION
LET'S ROLL

IT IS JULY 2009. We step off our respective planes and lug our gear into the sweltering Vegas sun. Our taxis creep through downtown tourist traffic, swing around the airport, and unceremoniously drop us off in a giant, industrial-looking parking lot.

The Las Vegas Sports Center sulks unimpressively in the heat, but under the sounds of arriving planes, there's also a low hum and periodic whistles. Inside, the air is cooler and smells vaguely of . . . what is that smell? Sweat? Feet? Happiness? And when our eyes adjust to the light, we see skaters from every corner of the world—their helmets whiz by in every direction looking as if they are floating on air. On their feet are skates—black skates, white skates, blue skates, camouflage skates—propelled by a rainbow of wheels.

On the sport floor, coaches with names like Carmen Getsome and Miss Fortune are drilling a centipede line of skaters in the fine art of knocking each other's asses to the ground. Refs and skaters gear up for the mixed league, multination, battle du jour: Team Australia vs. Team Canada. Someone hobbles by with an ice pack strapped to her knee, still smiling. We smile too.

Across town, nearly one thousand other skaters throng the

casino and head to seminars in the meeting halls of the Imperial Palace Hotel, with nothing but roller derby on their minds.

This is the fifth annual derby convention known as RollerCon. And, boy, have things changed in five years. We remember Roller-Con's inaugural year all too well. Back in that sweltering summer of 2005, there were just a few dozen leagues in existence, and all of them were here in the U.S. At the time, we spent most of the weekend meeting like-minded skaters, congratulating ourselves for finding the sport, and drinking cocktails in the pool. One of the most "official" events of the weekend was one the two of us organized: the utterly non-athletic Derby Wedding.

And who are we? Back in 2003, we were just Jenny Barbee and Alex Cohen, and we were both looking for something that was missing. Jenny was fresh off a disastrous dating debacle, and knew she needed a hobby to save her from a steady diet of Coronas and reality television. She found the L.A. Derby Dolls through her journalist friend Chris Nichols, and became Kasey Bomber.

Alex was a radio reporter who first heard about derby when a friend joined the then-burgeoning league in Texas. She spent a week hanging with rollergirls in Austin and then hankered to do derby herself when she returned to California. She saw one of the Derby Dolls' recruitment flyers at a local art gallery and, soon after, went to her first practice. Her ride, quite fortuitously, was Kasey Bomber. After one practice, Alex was officially hooked on the sport and became Axles of Evil.

And since then, not a week has gone by that we haven't worn our skates. It's filled us with great pride to watch and participate in this sport that has now grown to more than five hundred leagues in fifteen nations.

We can only imagine how much roller derby will evolve over the next five years, let alone the next five decades. And so we decided to take stock of this amazing sport's history and, hopefully, to help spread its gospel to those who have yet to come across it.

We by no means claim to have all the answers when it comes to derby. But we've been around a long time and have had the amazing honor of talking with many of the folks responsible for making it what it is today in all its many forms.

If there's one thing we've discovered in writing this book, it's that there is something universal about derby—be it banked track in Oklahoma or flat track in London. Skaters, derby girls, roller-girls, whatever you want to call us . . . come in all shapes and sizes, but our love for the sport is identical.

Watching roller derby today, you see the results of a rigorous training regimen and countless hours devoted to a labor of love. The end product before the ticket holder is hard hits and heroic athleticism, fun outfits, and clever names. But what's underneath are the girls who walked into their first practice, wide-eyed, nervous, and looking for something they had either lost or never had.

No matter how different one skater may look from another—how divided by race, socioeconomic status, age, or history—they share one thing in common: they are seekers. It's hunger that brings girls to this sport. Hunger for more . . . everything. And it's hunger that makes the game so damn exciting.

We sought, we worked, and we found. And like any good cult propagandists, we'd like to show you how you can, too.

L.A. DERBY DOLLS VENUE,
THE DOLL FACTORY

PHOTO BY MARC "STALKERAZZI" CAMPOS

What's It All A . . . . Bout?

IT'S A SATURDAY night in a neighborhood just west of downtown L.A. known as Historic Filipinotown or Hi-Fi. Nearly two thousand fans have traveled to a fifty-five-thousand-square-foot warehouse that once cranked out ice-cream cones—a place affectionately dubbed The Doll Factory. This is the home of the Los Angeles Derby Dolls—the city's all-girl, banked track, quad skate roller derby league.

Outside in the parking lot, gals in a red, yellow, and blue Hot Dog on a Stick truck sell corn dogs and lemonade. A local pizza parlor dishes out slices as a ska/punk band plays on a makeshift stage underneath a canopy of tall palm trees.

Among this crowd is just about every type of person you could hope to meet in Southern California. Heavily tattooed biker boys and hipster girls with bright blue hair mingle with grandmas in wheelchairs and young high-powered Hollywood types. There are die-hard muscle-bound sports fans and folks so un-athletically inclined they'd likely guess Yogi Berra was a cartoon character.

Stepping inside The Doll Factory is almost like that first color frame in *The Wizard of Oz*—where Dorothy finds herself transported to a marvelous world of Technicolor fantasy. Derby Dolls are everywhere—working the door, selling merch, wandering through

the bleachers with raffle tickets. True to their name, many of these women are dolled up—in team uniforms or other costumes, in bustiers and hot pants, in wigs or face paint. There is no shortage of fishnet stockings.

As a DJ plays thumping electro-punk in the background, vendors hawk necklaces made out of old soda caps, paintings of pin-up girls with skulls for faces, and t-shirts that read I'M NOT GAY, BUT MY DERBY WIFE IS. Bartenders do brisk sales out of rolling coolers filled with tall cans of Tecate beer, all bathed in the pink light of a four-foot-tall roller skate made of neon that hangs on the wall.

Suddenly, the lights dim and everyone flocks to the track, a beautiful one-hundred-by-sixty-foot wooden beast designed and built by skaters, friends, and family. It's shaped like the sort of track you likely ran on in school, but in this case the outer edges have been raised anywhere between three and five feet and propped up by a series of vertical rails and posts.

Fans crowd around every inch of the track and fill up bleachers and stands on all sides of it. Perched in a corner high above the track is a booth where two announcers introduce the two teams skating. On this night, the police-themed Sirens are facing off against the team that pays tongue-in-cheek homage to the Girl Scouts, the Tough Cookies.

The Sirens are dressed in dark blue skintight numbers no LAPD officer would dream of wearing while on patrol. The Tough Cookies are clad in short, pleated skirts and button-down uniform shirts adorned with badges for busting heads and breaking hearts.

Skaters have names like Paris Killton and Feara Nightly, Gori Spelling and Venus De Maul'r. They're fully covered in protective gear: helmets, mouth guards, elbow pads, wrist guards, knee pads . . . some even wear shin guards. They all move on roller skates as if they were born with wheels on their feet.

The crowd stands for the national anthem. At The Doll Factory, "The Star-Spangled Banner" has been performed by everyone from transgendered celebrity Alexis Arquette to a band of female kazoo players to Gene Simmons. Tonight it's an adorable local singer

VENUS DE MAUL'R FACES OFF
AGAINST MAGGIE MAYHEM

named Audra Mae with a sparkly smile and a voice like velvet. She belts the patriotic tune out like a modern day Bessie Smith.

By the time we get to "and the hooooooooooooooooome of the braaaaaaaaaaaaaaaaaave" the crowd is bouncing with excitement. The announcer, Evil E, ducks her head down to the microphone and asks the crowd, "Are you ready . . . for . . . *roller derby action*?" The audience explodes with wild screams as the moment they've all been waiting for finally arrives. Game on.

On a stretch of the track about six feet long, eight women—four from each team—position themselves in a group. They're crouched low, eyeing each other malevolently, bodies pressed together tightly—as if they're in an elevator built to fit only four. A whistle blows, and they take off together. As they skate, they slam their bodies against their opponents trying to knock each other over. This fierce and violent throng of women is called a pack.

WHAT'S IT ALL A . . . BOUT?

3

Moments later, a second whistle blows and two skaters poised behind the pack take off in a quick sprint. These skaters are the point scorers called jammers. The jammers charge toward the pack and do their best to skate through it. They try to juke and jive past hip-checks and through human walls of skaters lined shoulder to shoulder. Once the jammers make it out of the pack, they race around the track and approach the pack again—this time for points.

A jammer earns a point for each member of the opposite team she skates by after the first pass. That's why skaters in the pack try desperately to beat the living crap out of the jammer from the opposing team. They'll do just about anything to make sure she doesn't pick up any points. There are huge wallops, big spills, pile-ups, and collisions that make hockey look as tame as a round of nursing home shuffleboard.

And, there are points scored. Without any balls, bats, sticks, or nets, bouts are won and lost by the ability of women to pass each other on the track. Each time a jammer scores, the crowd goes insane.

At this Sirens/Cookies game, tension quickly mounts as each team takes turns eking out a small lead over the other. Finally, with just twenty-six seconds left on the clock, the Sirens are leading with a score of fifty-one to forty-eight. A guy dressed in a full body Cookie Monster suit runs back and forth in front of the bleachers—desperately trying to rally fans of his beloved namesake team.

And then, in the last few seconds of the game, the Tough Cookies pull it off, scoring enough points to win the game. The crowd rushes in, arms outstretched over the lip of the track, offering high-fives to skaters taking victory laps. The Sirens take a few laps too and the crowd is just as excited to cheer them on despite their defeat.

Afterward, skaters exit the track to give sweaty hugs to friends, family, and fans. Then it's off to the bar for the after-party, where derby girls prove they take their celebrating just as seriously as they do their skating.

This is the sport of roller derby. And despite the carnival-like atmosphere, it's an incredibly serious endeavor. There are countless adrenaline-filled moments. Strategies are beautifully executed by teams that have spent hours tirelessly training. Skaters execute breathtaking, eight-wheeled leaps; they fall thunderously and collide in ways that sometimes take them to the emergency room.

For those of us who skate, there are many reasons to love roller derby—the amazing friends, the outlet for creativity and aggression, the cardio-intensive exercise. But it's the bouts where all these amazing things come together, and that's what keeps us pouring so much of our time and energy into this sport year after year.

Nowadays, bouts are happening every weekend in just about every corner of the U.S. In New Orleans, the Big Easy Rollergirls have skated at Blaine Kern's Mardi Gras World, competing amidst ginormous King Kong and Mr. Bill parade floats. In the northern hills of New Mexico, the ladies of Duke City Derby skate at a community center in front of the majestic backdrop of the snow-covered mountains of Taos.

Derby has even gone global, with leagues sprouting up everywhere from Edmonton to Zurich and from Abu Dhabi to Copenhagen. Roller derby, as we know it today, is a distinctly twenty-first-century phenomenon. But the roots of this sport actually date back more than 125 years.

PROFiLE: Jackie Daniels

DOWN AND DERBY

PHOTO BY RYAN P PHOTO

There are people who find roller derby like a long lost friend. There are those who fall in love with the sport like they were dosed with Spanish Fly. And then there are those like Rachel Bockheim, a.k.a. Jackie Daniels.

In many ways, she's the quintessential derby girl—committed, tireless, talented, and well loved by her teammates and competitors alike. And when we say teammates, she sure does have a lot of those. In addition to skating with the Windy City Rollers in Chicago, she's also an original member of the Grand Raggidy Roller Girls of Grand Rapids, Michigan, as well as a part-time member of Team Awesome, Team Legit, and Michigan's Mitten Kittens. Like yellow and blue make green, combining Jackie and derby creates a new, magically kick-ass whole from the sum of its parts.

Q: *When did you start skating?*

JACKIE DANIELS: At our Catholic school annual outings. I think I went once since high school, and it was like riding a bike coming back. I operate better with skates on.

Q: *Did this kind of thing always appeal to you, or was roller derby a surprise?*

JD: Kinda both. I read an article about it, I knew it was for me, but at that point, I was living in Grand Rapids and didn't know the town was just starting a team. I knew Chicago was just starting and I honestly considered moving to Chicago back then so I could play. As soon as I knew about derby, I knew I was going to play no matter what.

Q: *What are some of the things besides the skating that you really enjoy about derby?*

JD: I love the people, I love the parties, and I love learning new things. I have met my best friends here, I have had the time of my life so many times at roller derby events, and I have grown as a person and professional by the things I've learned and challenges I've overcome. I couldn't imagine my life without this.

Q: What are some of the advantages of playing on teams like Team Awesome and Team Legit, which are made up of skaters from multiple leagues?

JD: Learning, travel, and fun with friends are the huge draws for me. Every time I would play with one of these teams, I could bring back valuable lessons for myself and my home league. When my home league isn't able to travel as much as I would like, I can fulfill that desire on other teams. And, it's such a blast being surrounded by exciting new people that have the same obsession, passion, and drive for roller derby. All have the same goal, no drama, and an overwhelming desire to play more—it creates an unbelievable environment of excitement.

Q: Over the past year, how many times have you traveled for derby?

JD: I played, attended, or coached at twenty events outside of my base camp in 2009.

Q: How exactly do you maintain the energy to be involved with so many teams?

JD: I create busy. If I don't have something to work on (even for like five minutes), I'll make a project, a task. I'll decide something our league needs to perfect or change and start working on that. I am a firm believer that you can do anything you put your mind to, and I never give up. I truly want to see roller derby, my league, and myself succeed. So I keep doing anything and everything I can to keep pushing us all forward. I am a perfectionist who is never satisfied . . . just ask my exes.

Q: *Who is your roller derby idol or derby crush?*

JD: Teflon Donna from Philly Roller Girls, she hip-whipped off me early on (it was my first) and I've loved her ever since!

Q: *When the day to retire comes, what do you think will be the most valuable thing you'll take away from your experience with derby?*

JD: If I don't skate, how could I justify eating and drinking like this?! To be honest, I am really not sure retirement will come for me. I'll be playing in the Grandma Games 2050. Or, perhaps I'll transition to coaching. I think I will continually be involved in derby in some capacity, to continue learning and having the time of my life.

The First Whistle

ROLLER DERBY IS like the cat of the sports' animal kingdom. No matter how hard the sport falls, it always seems to land on its feet. Every time it appears derby is dead—it somehow pounces back into claw-bearing action. It's already been through several lives and we're fairly certain there are quite a few more ahead of it. We've trolled the archives of many newspapers, magazines, and Frank Deford's incredible book *Five Strides on the Banked Track: The Life and Times of the Roller Derby* to help compile this lesson in our beloved sport's early origin.

The first recognized incarnation of this multi-lived minx dates back nearly eighty years, to the Great Depression. Yes, if there was anything remotely "great" about the Depression, it's that it was an era when roller derby as we know it took its first tentative lap.

In the 1930s, an American had to be creative in order to earn a buck or two. People were poor, and they were desperate. And where there is desperation, there are always crafty people ready to capitalize on it.

These were the days of dance marathons, where promoters pushed contestants to their physical limits. Couples would clutch and sway for days at a time in an attempt to outlast their rivals and earn just enough money to feed their families.

At the same time, a new and happier pastime's popularity was booming: roller skating. For mere cents on the dollar, the youth of the world could woo each other wearing high-laced boots fitted with screechy metal or, slightly preferable, scratchy wood wheels, skating counter-clockwise around rinks to the most popular pipe organ music of the day. Along with other such sinful activities as walking in parks and attending those new talking pictures at the movie house, roller skating rinks took off as the hub of teenage activity.

It didn't take long before someone put two and two together and realized the marathon dancing fad and the roller skating craze could work well together. That man was a former film distributor named Leo Seltzer.

Seltzer started by promoting "derbies"—marathon races with partners trading off laps on a banked track until they either successfully skated the equivalent of the distance between New York, and Los Angeles or collapsed from bloody feet and/or exhaustion.

But these early incarnations of Seltzer's brand of roller derby were not entirely original. In fact, they were actually a more extreme incarnation of roller skating races that had been creating controversy in New York as early as 1885.

NINETEENTH CENTURY SKATING: ROLLER RACES

On March 2, 1885, Madison Square Garden played host to the debut of an unprecedented six-day skating marathon. Men arrived from all over the world to strap on skates and test their endurance to the limit—or well beyond it. Stories that month in *The New York Times* revealed the public zeal throughout the race as nineteen-year old William Donovan of Elmira, New York, pulled into a handy lead to win. It was a remarkable feat for a young man who almost missed the contest altogether when his skates were stolen. In six days, he skated a record-breaking 1,092 miles, covering up to 204 miles in a single day!

But a week later, Donovan would be dead.

Against the advice of both his trainer and doctor, Donovan's father removed him from bed rest only two days after the tournament in order to make some extra money on public appearances. Donovan showed signs of strain, and was soon too sick to stand. While he struggled for his life, the public was shocked and saddened by the death of another young race entrant—Joseph Cohen. Officials ruled that Cohen's death was caused by "meningitis, aggravated, if not induced, by prolonged excitement of body and mind, and also by exposure consequent upon his participation in a six-day roller-skating match."

In Donovan's case reports suggested that he left his sick bed to watch the passing of the P.T. Barnum Circus parade outside his window and moments later, succumbed to "acute pericarditis" exacerbated by the exertions of the race.

Suddenly the early excitement for the sport had turned into a tide of anger and public outrage. Roller skating, it seemed, was a killer of vital young men—a wheeled devil sent to tempt the young into vice, with fatal consequences. After a follow-up race failed to attract a crowd, one *New York Times* editorialist described the dire gravity of the entire skating pastime in a piece on May 18 of that year. "Elopements, betrayals, bigamous marriages, and other social transgressions," the writer suggested, "were traced to the association of the innocent with the vicious upon the skating floor." Furthermore, the writer asserted, "the rink is too often a place where good-looking scoundrels do a great deal of harm."

Many predicted that such bad press would spell the end of not just derbies, but roller skating itself.

SELTZER AND THE FEMALE FACTOR

Periodic races held at Madison Square Garden over the next fifty years proved those predictions false. Races continued virtually unchanged, cropping up every decade or so. While Leo Seltzer may not have invented the endurance race, he was a man who understood the value of a good hook and angle. So, when Seltzer debuted his version of roller derby on August 13, 1935, at the Chicago Coliseum, he forever changed the sport by introducing two key elements: spectacle and women.

Seltzer realized the tradition of all-male sports was missing out on some key audience demographics: female. And what better way to reach the women of America than to include them as competitors? From all over the country, women traveled to Seltzer's Chicago hub, partnered with their sons, brothers, husbands, and fathers, for the opportunity to be a part of his newly named Transcontinental Roller Derby.

One of these women was Josephine "Ma" Bogash, an already middle-aged, no-nonsense broad who dragged along her son Billy. Known to sometimes carry a large hatpin in her hair, Ma would slide it out during a traffic jam on the track and, unseen by the refs, stick her surprised competitors to get them out of the way. Underhanded, you say? Absolutely! But the audience loved her, as well as her fresh-faced son. Race after race, Bogash fans filled seats to see what the duo would do next. Ma Bogash's fiery demeanor and skill on skates gave Seltzer the first indication that "personality players" were the ticket-selling wave of the future.

As anyone who participates in derby today can tell you, combining sport and femininity is a double-edged sword. It was no different in the early days. While the women attracted a whole

MA AND BILLY BOGASH MUG FOR THE CAMERA

PHOTO COURTESY OF THE ROLLER DERBY HALL OF FAME

new audience, it also resulted in skepticism from the media. How could female skaters actually be both womanly and athletic? Who wants to see women doing manly things in manly places? Why, the next thing you know, they'll want to go out and get jobs and wear pants to church!

In other words, while women finally had publicly recognized role models in the world of sports, others were hell-bent on dismissing their participation as a sideshow novelty. That was merely the first battle in a war that still continues raging today. But like it or leave it, the Transcontinental Roller Derby brought co-ed competition into the world, and it was here to stay.

In the initial Transcontinental Derby races, co-ed pairs skated laps around an oval track. First, men would skate a number of laps while their female partner rested, and then they would switch. Though Seltzer reportedly began staging his races on the traditional flat oval track, he eventually returned to a banked one, because tired, out of control skaters had a tendency to end up sprawling into the audiences' laps. Ironically, today, this very brand of "audience participation" has become one of the most gleeful arguments in favor of modern flat track roller derby.

To add excitement to the long lasting endurance laps, exhausted skaters would be expected to periodically stop mid-stride to compete in short sprinting races or "jams." Because these jams were quick bursts of speed that resulted in immediate cash winnings, these races often got fierce. Brawling and falling reached new heights, because the skaters would stop at nothing to finish first.

One notable member of the audience to witness some of this down-and-dirty strategizing was a popular newsman of the day named Damon Runyon. Runyon noticed that polite audiences turned into a pack of rafter-raising heathens when the bodies hit the floor. At a dinner with Seltzer and friends in 1938, Runyon suggested that Seltzer incorporate this human pinball action and strategy into a more structured co-ed sport. Over the course of that meal, legend has it, the modern game of roller derby was born amid scratches and doodles on a napkin.

TIME OUT!

Dark Days for Derby: No One's Number One

JUST AS ROLLER DERBY was seizing the world as a new and exciting team sport, it nearly met its end. On March 24, 1937, in Salem, Illinois, a bus filled with skaters and support staff was traveling from St. Louis to Cincinnati when the front tire reportedly experienced a blow out. Driver Dick Thomas attempted to correct the vehicle's violent swerving but was unable to avoid crashing into a bridge abutment.

Several ushers who were traveling behind the bus in their own cars witnessed the accident and said that the bus "appeared to explode" when it tipped over after the collision. Of the twenty-three passengers on the bus, only four survived, and none escaped serious injury. Leo Seltzer was called upon to provide a list of the deceased. With sadness, he named ten of his renowned skaters, and nine members of the league's support staff, including a registered nurse, a chiropractor, and two concessions operators.

Typical of the disposition of Seltzer's crew, anecdotal history has it that while in the hospital succumbing to severe injuries from the crash, Ted Mullen, Roller Derby's master of ceremonies asked the doctor, "Do you think I'll ever be able to skate?" The doctor assured him that he would. To which, Mullen responded through his pain,

THE FIRST WHISTLE

15

"Funny, I never was able to before." Not long after this final punch line, Mullen joined the list of fatalities.

The effect the crash had on the derby community was not unlike the aftershocks from the plane crash that took the lives of Buddy Holly, Richie Valens, and the Big Bopper two decades later. The devastation to the sport and its fans was immeasurable. In response to the tragedy, jersey number one was forever retired in honor of the skaters who were lost.

Rumor had it, however, that before number one was retired out of respect, it was already considered bad luck. Around the same time as the bus crash, amidst a fast and furious game, skater Stewart Erwin, who wore number one, tripped on the inside edge of the track, which was slightly elevated from the arena floor. Though similar falls had taken place before, and have taken place countless times since, Irwin's fall represented the worst-case scenario. After returning to finish the game, Erwin later died of unrealized internal injuries. In the nearly eighty years of roller derby as we know it, his was the only fatality during a game. But, in typical show-must-go-on fashion, the dangerous inner edge of the track was lowered so it was flush with the floor and the derby continued the next day.

ON THE STARTING LINE

Along the road to creating the new sport, however, there were some strange and hilarious sidetracks.

At one point, rather than two teams, Seltzer tried three teams on the track, all competing at once. Imagine a football game with three teams facing off at the same time. If the term "mayhem," or something less polite, comes to mind when you try to picture fifteen skaters duking it out with each other simultaneously, you get the picture.

Leo Seltzer was desperately looking for ways to fill the seats, and as a promoter, he wasn't above asking his skaters to give a little extra for the fans. Audiences in Des Moines were privy to probably the strangest promotion in derby history when they turned on their radios in 1938 to find a broadcast of the Roller Derby skaters playing basketball (on skates) against the Harlem Globetrotters.

Though a basketball game against the Globetrotters was pure insanity, the comparison to those famous showmen wasn't altogether crazy. In many ways, the structure of the early roller derby league had a lot in common with how the Globetrotters worked. Their travels took them all over the country, to cities like Cincinnati, St. Louis, and Louisville. When they arrived at their next destination, skaters would split up into a "home" team and a team of "visitors," each geared toward the part of the country they were in. If the skaters were in Nebraska, for instance, the home team would immediately become the Omaha Something-or-others, and the visitors would represent a frightening, evil, big city, such as New York.

But even if they clashed like titans on the track, the two opposing teams shared traveling arrangements, hotel lodging, and locker rooms. Men, women, trainers, announcers, and officials were all one big happy family, sometimes literally. Since their schedule allowed very little social time outside the confines of their charter bus, intra-league romances were not uncommon.

What's more, while these skaters may have been professional athletes, their salary didn't come in the form of a bi-weekly paycheck, fancy cars, fur coats, and an entourage. Paid in food, shelter, and the opportunity to see the world, they were quite literally broke. Never mind that in Roller Derby the definition of the "world" was Bangor, Lincoln, and Pittsburgh—travel was still a bonus for these kids.

And with some notable exceptions, most of the skaters were just that—kids. What many of them lacked in education, they made up for in desire, hope, and energy. With the derby, they got a family, three square meals a day, and, even better, admiration and applause.

Much of that applause went to the personality players like Ma and Billy Bogash. Promoter Leo Seltzer began recognizing their potential as crowd-pleasers and started developing and promoting rivalries between the skaters. Sure, the audience loved a good fall, but it was positively itching for a good fight, especially if that fight was between two women. Derby found its first perfect rivalry in the match up of Midge "Toughie" Brasuhn and Gerry Murray.

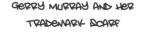

GERRY MURRAY AND HER
TRADEMARK SCARF

MIDGE "TOUGHIE"
BRASUHN SOFTENS
UP WITH HER SON

DOWN AND DERBY

TOUGHY VS. GERRY

Sixteen-year-old Gerry Murray was a glamorous and pretty high school dropout from Des Moines, Iowa, who joined Roller Derby in 1938. Toughie, the rough-and-tumble fifteen-year-old daughter of a St. Paul, Minnesota, plumber, joined in 1941. Murray was deemed the sweetheart pin-up girl of derby, and even today you can occasionally find evidence of her popularity when trademarked "Gerry Murray Hair Bows" appear on eBay. Toughie, in contrast, stood out as a tough-talking four-foot-eleven thug, making up for her lack of glamour with an endless reservoir of pure and scrappy determination.

It was a classic case of good versus evil, only with a whole lot of gray area in between, where hair pulling, sneaky fists to the ribs, and tripping resided. Murray was sneaky, but smilingly charming—a wolf in Betty Grable's clothing. Toughie was brutal, but in a nakedly apparent way that resulted in a season-long, hilariously stormy relationship with the penalty box. Their clashes were legendary, and the fans loved the blue-collar justice of their brawls. In fact, the audience became so passionate along Murray/Toughie partisan lines that a female fan once reportedly threw her baby at Toughie in the heat of outrage. Luckily, Toughie, quick on the draw, caught the infant and returned the child safely to its slightly less-agitated father.

WHOA TELLY!

Toughie Brasuhn and Gerry Murray were still some of the main attractions of the roller derby when it met head-on with another revolutionary innovation of the time: television. In the late 1940s, TV sets were still going for about $745 so the average American household hadn't quite joined the club yet. Additionally, Kinescope cameras used for filming programs were large and cumbersome, lighting was prohibitively expensive, and as a result, there wasn't much in terms of programming. Roller Derby, with its stage-like track and dynamic action provided a unique opportunity to fill some of the hours of dead air for the CBS network.

With an initial thirteen-week contract, television and derby first combined forces to broadcast a New York Chiefs versus Brooklyn Red Devils game from the 69th Regiment Armory in Manhattan. On November 29, 1948, the game was aired in a prime time slot and attracted an impressive share of viewing attention. That's not too much of a surprise considering competing programs included the opening of the Metropolitan Opera, "film shorts," and a program called "Court of Popular Opinion: Should Religion be Taught in Our Public Schools."

Thus the occasionally abusive romance between Roller Derby and television began. With television's thirst for programming to fill every hour of the day, Derby's presence on the boob tube was overwhelming. By 1949, the sport had hit new heights of popularity. The playoffs that year sold out more than nineteen thousand seats at Madison Square Garden each night for a whole week running.

ABC, Derby's new network, knew a good thing when it rolled over their fingers. Because the sport was so theatrical and relatively easy to film, ABC started plugging Derby bouts into every available space. Eventually, bouts were broadcast up to four or five times a week. Leo Seltzer was worried about overexposure, and rightfully so.

Despite Seltzer's earnest pleas that ABC cut down the number of bouts aired each week—suggesting Friday nights and Sunday afternoons as good family entertainment time—ABC kept on truckin' full speed. As proof of the network's lack of pre-NFL savvy, they famously retorted that no sports would *ever* be played on Sundays!

In 1950, at the height of its heyday, Seltzer's Roller Derby expanded to six teams. But by 1951, Roller Derby was off the air. The jaded public was no longer tuning in, and even Seltzer himself was almost ready to tune out. Disillusioned with the trajectory of his sport, Seltzer handed the franchise over to his son Jerry in 1958. The era of Ma Bogash, Toughie, and Gerry was coming to a close.

CALIFORNIA STOMPING GROUND

That same year, Jerry Seltzer packed up the track, and like countless migrants before him, looked for gold in the sunshine of the West Coast. Setting up camp in San Francisco, Jerry made the San Francisco Bay Bombers his go-to team for a revitalized league that would eventually feature ten teams and over two hundred skaters.

His new crew was up to a running start with new, outrageous, and bigger-than-life personality skaters, such as Joanie "Blonde Bomber" Weston and her foil, the legendary Ann "Demon of the Derby" Calvello. Complementing these gals were male superstars like Charlie O'Connell and Ronnie Robinson (boxer Sugar Ray Robinson's son). The Bay Area came out in droves, often outselling even local Oakland Raiders games.

JOAN WESTON THE "BLONDE BOMBER," THE GOLDEN GIRL OF THE BAY

Joanie Weston Versus Ann Calvello—Get Your Tickets

BLONDE, CHARMING, AND 6′3″ on wheels, Joan Weston was a seventeen-year-old surfer girl when she answered the call of Roller Derby. When Derby came to San Francisco in the 1950s, Joanie was a shoe-in with her strapping California-girl looks and naturally nurturing personality. Within a few short years, she was the go-to team captain for the girls of the Bombers. By the 1960s, Weston was the highest paid female athlete in the world.

With her trademark golden waves and pink scarf catching the draft of her speed, she held the Bay Area audience in thrall with a quick smile and a quicker hip-check. Darling of the track she may have been, but Weston was no shrinking violet. She threw down with the best of them, tirelessly lapping the competition and tangling in legendary brawls with her rival, Ann Calvello. It seemed Weston could do anything. So much so that in her rare off-season time, she picked up world championship trophies as an open water canoeist in Hawaii!

Like Toughie Brasuhn, Ann Calvello provided the perfect foil for the glamorous Blonde Bomber persona of Weston. With her rainbow-colored hairstyles, sassy quips, and wild make-up, Calvello is remembered by derby girls of today as their rough-hewn role model—punk rock before Sid Vicious could even buy smokes. Calvello joined Derby in New York in 1948, and competed professionally in the sport in each of the next seven decades. As far as role models go, there could be no better.

Twelve broken noses, four broken elbows, a broken collarbone, a broken tailbone, and blindness in one eye never broke Calvello's spirit for the game she loved. She held the crowd as surely as Joanie did, but with delicious antagonism and sharp wit. She famously referred to her breasts as "tickets," citing her and the other girls' assets as the main reason men filled the seats. Off track, the self-named Lioness was actually a sweet and kind woman who hoped everyone's final assessment agreed that she was "a good broad."

Today, the spirit of Weston and Calvello burns bright in new players. For example, there's Dee Bomb and Blonde An'bitchin. These platinum-tressed sisters in the Oly Rollers of Olympia, Washington, are referred to as "The Ponytails" by their rivals. The Ponytails are like the athletic godchildren of Weston. On the other hand, Calvello's urban hellion roots run deep in the demonic speed of Suzy Hotrod of New York's Gotham Girls and the outrageous warpaint of Demanda Riot of the Bay Area Derby Girls. Every time a girl takes a lap today, it is with thanks to Weston and loud loving boos to Calvello, who wouldn't have it any other way.

In the meantime, television came knocking for a second date. The bouquet it pulled from behind its back this time was a lightweight little gem called a video camera. With the relative mobility of that device, Roller Derby returned to the airwaves with the magic of syndication. Games could now be taped and aired in any order, on any station, at any time of day. The upside was cheap and easy programming. The downside was that wins and losses were insignificant without an actual season.

Local fans in San Francisco also learned that geography was meaningless, because not only the Bombers, but also the New York Chiefs and the Chicago Pioneers were actually based in San Francisco! Like the early days, once again the Visitors were usually culled from the same general pool of skaters as the Home team. In these days, Joanie Weston was the golden girl captain of the hometown Bombers, and Ann Calvello was shooting out her hips and shooting off her mouth for the villainous Visitors. And just as with Toughie and Murray before them, everyone loved a good catfight.

For several years, derby did well in syndication. So well, in fact, that another outfit begun in Los Angeles by Bill Griffiths, Sr. hit the scene with the hometown L.A. T-Birds. Roller Games—Griffiths's more theatrical style of the sport—was met with disdain by the traditional derby skaters, who still favored a more athletic slant. But the Roller Games drew good crowds.

CLASH OF THE TITANS CHARLIE O'CONNELL FACES OFF AGAINST MIKE GAMMON

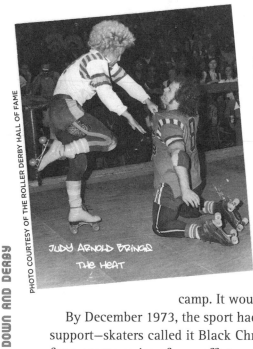

JUDY ARNOLD BRINGS THE HEAT

Syndication of both leagues' bouts continued and fans followed until the early 1970s. That's when a gas crisis and a skaters' union strike spelled the end for Seltzer's original traveling roller carnival.

In 1972, disillusioned by the increase in theatricality and fixed incomes, Jerry Seltzer folded his roller derby operation. In its wake, some remaining skaters migrated to Griffiths's Roller Games camp. It would be a short stay.

By December 1973, the sport had once again lost its television support—skaters called it Black Christmas. Though some held on for a sparse series of one-off games over the next few years, the sun had officially set on Derby's second golden age.

The Spandex Years

BY THE 1980s, roller derby was hobbling along like a toothless bear without a circus. Skaters were playing in the occasional expo bouts, but the crowds were thinning, and awareness of the sport was fading.

But in 1986, derby's estranged baby daddy, ABC, came knocking once again. Looking for something flashy to pair with the massive popularity of late-night televised wrestling, not to mention a contender to squash the fifteen-year stranglehold on weekend TV held by rival NBC's *Saturday Night Live*, roller derby seemed like the perfect ally.

The network's bright idea was a night featuring overly muscled, sleekly-spandexed lunkheads, battling for some kind of macho honor in the form of *American Gladiators*. This would be followed by a second hour counterpart called *Rock-n-Roller-games*—a version of roller derby that came complete with a Wall of Death, a pit of live alligators, and an original soundtrack that would make Kenny Loggins cry bearded tears.

Bill Griffiths and his brand of derby were running the game once again. And as silly as the spandex bike-short-inspired uniforms they wore may look today, the game was not without its share of fun and kitschy flair. The traditional oval track was forsaken for a pumped-up figure eight, with a heavily banked turn resembling something Tony Hawk might have dreamed up on an acid trip. In the center, there was even a ramp to add extra exclamation points to the "Holy Crap!!" design.

Co-ed competitors combined daredevil vert-skating stunts with high-speed, acrobatic collisions. Leapfrogs, full-body clotheslines, and mid-air crunches were par for the course. Pack action was so outrageous that viewers almost expected a giant Batman-style "POW!" to appear at any moment.

The skills and spills of the diminutive skater Ralphy Valladares and other veterans of the old game still garnered applause. However, newer, younger skaters with bigger hair and puffier egos seemed more bent on getting air time than catching air. In true Roller Games fashion, the real-life, mind-boggling athletic skill of the skaters was consistently overshadowed by overblown, laughable WWF-style fights on the infield.

And, as if those human shenanigans weren't enough, there was also the alligator pit. If a game resulted in a tie, the audience would be gradually cloaked in sexy, manufactured smoke. Out of the murk, scantily clad "Alligator Dancers" gyrated to a song warning that "the roller gator's gonna get you, better run, better hide . . . ."

Two men resembling oily, shaved apes then carried two live gators to the pit, and beckoned the masked "gator skaters" to begin their match race. The first skater to successfully lap the gator pit five times or push the other skater into the pit would gain the winning point for their team. Would you like to guess how that usually turned out? Yep, nothing says roller derby like a round of gator wrasslin'. Though skaters and producers of *Rock-n-Rollergames* were insistent on promoting the action as being legitimate and totally spontaneous, the all-too-predictable gator pit action made the sport look about as real as Pamela Anderson's knockers.

Entertaining though it may have been, *Rock-n-Rollergames* only lasted for one season. The spandex, however, couldn't be so easily dismissed.

Fast forward to the nineties, a decade the skating community could aptly call the Era of the Rollerblade. Gone were the supple, broken-in leather speed skates, and in their place came the unwieldy, hard plastic devices known as "fruit boots" to sneering traditionalists. Despite the fact that even Cindy Crawford couldn't make these wheeled ski boots sexy, the craze was a veritable explosion. To the annoyance of skateboarders and rink rats everywhere, 'bladers were hitting the skate parks, swarming the boardwalks, and reviving the dying roller rinks across the world.

The Nashville Network (TNN), then best known for its devotion to corny *Hee Haw* reruns, was trying to revamp its hayseed image at the time. These new, hot doohickeys were just what they needed, or so they thought. Cue spandex, a banked track, and a new generation of "sexy" young skaters, and you've got yourself *RollerJam.*

RollerJam had its heart in the right place in the beginning. In development for a 1999 premiere, producers reunited the sport with Jerry Seltzer, who owned the Roller Derby league from 1958 to 1972, and served as "commissioner" for this new league.

Skaters were auditioned across the country—speed skate champions and even third generation derby skaters were recruited to guarantee maximum action. They secured a soundstage at Universal Studios in Orlando and attempted a top-notch production. Gone were the alligators and the dancers, in their place was "sports entertainment" designed to balance the best of both worlds.

Despite initial enthusiasm, however, something went wrong. Footage of *RollerJam* bouts reveals a sparsely populated set of soundstage box seats more suited to a Sotheby's auction than a blue-collar brawl. This definitely did not look like the kind of audience that would throw a baby at a skater! Or, maybe the problem was simply that in-line skates never looked cool or tough. Despite hard hits and amazing feats, despite muscles and deep California tans, skaters still looked like figure skaters at a heavy metal show.

PROFILE: Quadzilla

Hockey skating, dance skating, aggressive skating, jam skating . . . you name it, Mo Sanders does it. Watching him skate derby is a bit like watching Baryshnikov on wheels—he leaps, he twists, he tour jetés his way through a pack. Oh, and did we mention he does all this wearing skates that are barely tied on to his feet?

Mo grew up with skating in his blood—his dad, a firefighter in Tacoma, Washington, was known to skate back and forth to work. Mo's currently a coach with the Rat City Rollergirls. But back in the day, he was one of the star players on the TNN show *RollerJam*.

Q: *You're known by many names . . . Barack O'Trauma, Quadzilla, Quadzilla LK. What's the LK about?*

MO SANDERS: Roller skating acted as a babysitter for us growing up. Your parents would drop you off at the rink on Saturday night at six o'clock, give you ten bucks, and pick you up at midnight. It was a safe place to go because all your friends and cousins and relatives were all there.

I was mostly self-taught, a real rink rat, but one of the owners of the rink where I used to skate would help me out. Her name was Lanny Werner and she was an artistic skater, a national champion. People used to call me

Lanny's Kid (LK) because she took me under her wing. She was a little short white lady and her husband was a seven-foot-tall basketball player from Washington State University. So people were pretty perplexed when he'd say, "Yeah this is me and Lanny's kid" and this short black kid would roll up.

Q: *How'd you get involved in* RollerJam*?*

MS: I used to skate a bunch down in California. One of the girls I skated with at Venice Beach was doing *RollerJam* in Florida. She's the one who told me they were hiring skaters. *RollerJam* had some roller derby people from the sixties and seventies and they were slowly grabbing up all kinds of other skaters: people off the boardwalk, roller hockey skaters, so my friend thought I would be good for it.

I went to auditions and wound up doing four seasons with the show.

Q: *What was that like?*

MS: I liked it a lot. I learned a whole lot of stuff from a bunch of people who were founding members of Roller Derby in its heyday. But, it was also kind of crazy and chaotic. They were throwing a lot of money at people to come out to Florida and put on this TV show. But the show was kind of like *World Wide Wrestling*. They had scripts, so it wasn't like it was a fully competitive, legit competition to see who was the best skater. You knew who was going to win. You knew how many points were going to be scored. You knew who was going to get into the fights—that part was really weird.

Q: *You had been a professional athlete for years at that point, so how was it doing staged games?*

MS: Well of course it sucked. According to the organizers, my job was to sell the other skater. So me being the skater that I am, and having the abilities I have, I was pretty miserable having to go out there and make somebody else look good when they were horrible. I could go out there and smash people all day long. I'm faster than a lot of the other people I skated with, and I know that if somebody hits me I'm not necessarily going to go down the way I made it look on TV. . . .

So it was hard doing *RollerJam* because it's tough to hold back and say, "Okay, I'll let this guy win," when you know deep inside you could kick this guy's ass all over the place. But for the sake of getting a paycheck, you couldn't really do that.

Q: *I understand you had some interesting hairdos at the time. . . .*

MS: I used to do all sorts of crazy stuff. I had platinum hair with the red and black leopard spots. I would do tiger stripes or stars or something. I would shave things in my head like crop circles.

Q: RollerJam *didn't last too long. Why do you think that is?*

MS: They didn't have a very good fan base, and I think it was just too hokey. There was too much drama, too much scripting. When your highest ratings come out of Biloxi, Mississippi . . . well, let's just say, I don't see that as being one of the hottest markets for TV.

Q: *Some people are trying to bring this current version of roller derby to television. How do you think it would fare?*

MS: It would probably get a bigger following than *RollerJam* did because roller derby has crossed over into mainstream America. Now it's like we all play this sport. The women skating today are your wives, your moms, your girlfriends, your sisters, and it not just a bunch of muscle heads rolling around doing a show. It's an actual sport. It isn't scripted, it's legitimate, and it has rules.

Seeing how many people are doing derby across the planet, I think a TV show could do well, especially if the producers don't try to take too much control, and just let the girls do their thing.

Whatever it was that slowed down *RollerJam*, producers became increasingly desperate to keep up the ratings. The formerly impressive athleticism soon took a backseat to fake personality conflicts, beauty over brawn, and the phoniest fights ever witnessed in the sport, which is saying a lot.

With their catfights and hair pulling, "The Bod Squad," a group of Barbie-esque amazons led by super-blonde Stacey Blitsch overshadowed the more skilled men. Costumes became increasingly skimpy, and the side-plots as tangled as a telenovela.

While these new derby men and women may have been great skaters, great actors they were not. Fans of melodrama went elsewhere, and fans of the sport reached for the remote.

And so it was that roller derby's latest incarnation came to a close in 2001. But, like with any good fighter, it takes more than a few punches to keep this sport down. Somewhere deep in the heart of Texas, as the *RollerJam* skaters were hanging up their spandex, a wannabe Svengali named Devil Dan met with some very strong-willed and tenacious women. Over beer and burgers, they were developing a plan for an all-new brand of wheeled world domination.

A DEAL WITH THE DEVIL

January 11, 2001, Austin, Texas. A long-established hangout on Austin's famous Sixth Street called Casino El Camino—a bar whose jukebox is as tasty as its burgers—was about to play host to an odd assembly. Waiting at the bar was Dan Policarpo, a young sidewinder who called himself "Devil Dan." He was holding a flyer he'd made in a fit of lightning inspiration and posted around town. Devil Dan was ready to breathe life back into roller derby. He'd used the posters to get the word out, and now he was waiting to meet some of his recruits.

April Ritzenthaler, a blonde masseuse as intelligent as she is attractive, was one of the first girls to arrive. She expected to see a few of her friends and ten, maybe twelve, local girls showing up to see what Devil Dan had to say. As the meeting time arrived, however, she was floored to see the crowd swell to nearly fifty women.

Also in attendance was Rachelle Moore, a lanky twenty-something with an easy smile. Moore had an athletic background and ties to the skateboard community. She found herself immediately attracted to the idea of roller derby, because, unlike other male-dominated sports, she notes, "When I closed my eyes and thought about derby, I automatically pictured a girl."

With their, and a hundred other, eager, slightly skeptical eyes on him, Dan held up a chicken-scratched piece of paper, not unlike Runyan and Seltzer's infamous napkin of yore, and rattled off his outlandish Burning Man–esque plan.

"There's gonna be live music, midgets, fire breathers, and multimedia presentations, all sponsored by bars, that will battle it out through roller derby," he proclaimed. "We're all gonna be superstars!"

He suggested that this girls-only league divide into four teams according to which bars each person frequented. Ritzenthaler helmed the Casino el Camino lot, thereafter dubbed the Putas del Fuego. Tattooed ironworker Nancy Haggerty took charge of the hot rod–themed Hellcats. Amanda Hardison created the gang of naughty Catholic schoolgirls that would be called the Holy Rollers. And since this was Texas, it's little surprise that one team was dubbed the Rhinestone Cowgirls. That team went to Anya Jack, who already sported a cowgirl tattoo.

Excitement was fever-pitched as the women continued recruiting and tested out some wheels for the first time. Skating hopefuls adopted new noms de guerre that would play on either their personalities or the super-heroic alter egos they embodied in their most satisfying fantasies. Local bartender Amy Sherman re-emerged as the glam-rock heroine Electra Blu. Charismatic Latina Sara Luna, on skates, became Lunatic. Statuesque Teresa Pappas would become Bettie Rage, an action/adventure variation on pin-ups past. Rachelle Moore mined comic strips, and became the deceptively sweet-sounding Sparkle Plenty. April Ritzenthaler, captain of the Putas, was La Muerta, Queen Destroyer.

But, before these newly named warriors could start rolling, they needed money. With $1,500 seed money gleaned from area bars and businesses, they planned a March fundraiser replete with raucous local bands and rowdy roller-hopefuls. Expectations were high. But on the night of the event, Devil Dan, league purser, among other things, showed up empty handed. Somewhere along the line, the girls report, the money had disappeared

THE GIRLS OF BGGW SPREAD THE DERBY GOSPEL WITH FLYERS

into thin air. Or, as popular opinion suggests, into Dan's bloodstream. Soon after, Dan vanished from Austin entirely, only to resurface years later in Tulsa, Oklahoma.

Though Dan might tell the story differently, the betrayal was devastating to the derby hopefuls at the time. But occasionally, good things arrive in unexpected fashion. The idea of making this derby thing work had rooted so deeply into the hearts of these Austin women that they were not prepared to give it up. And while Dan may have initially been behind the derby renaissance, hailing him as responsible for the current incarnation of the sport would be a far cry from the truth. As La Muerta says, "Devil Dan brought the matches, but we provided the flame."

ROLLING

What remained in the wake of Dan's departure was a group that was driven, but one that lacked most of the skills necessary to form a successful derby league, such as the ability to skate. "It was just party girls hanging out in bars and talking about something that may or may not happen," Sparkle Plenty recalls of the first few months. "We did more drinking than we did skating."

And considering that successful models for roller derby leagues were almost nonexistent at that time, the group was forced to wing it entirely. Bob Ray, who was filming the women at the time for a documentary called *Hell on Wheels*, notes that "they were kind of creating derby as they remembered it, which wasn't always derby the way it actually had been in reality." From a recollection skewed by youthful idealism and media input, these pioneering skaters reincarnated the sport as a cross between the hard hits of Saturday afternoon Weston versus Calvello brawls and the fashion bonanza of Farrah Fawcett duking it out on skates in *Charlie's Angels*. "Farrah looked hot on skates," Ray adds, "So in their vision, roller derby was hot as well. It wasn't about those weird, unsexy uniforms the women used to really wear."

In search of skating advice, these derby upstarts skulked around open skates at Skate World, a local rink, hoping to snag some skills from the experienced jam skaters that frequented the floor. They eventually joined forces with a figure skating coach who had expertise and agility, but was short on the skills particular to derby. There had to be a better way.

The more experienced skaters, such as Olivia "Cherry Chainsaw" Dansfiell, a former figure skater, helped the newbies' technique by sharing skills and insight. And Sparkle Plenty's day job teaching young children found a surprising practical use in her role as training coordinator for the league. The group was comprised of rowdy, opinionated, brash women not used to being corralled by a coach or following strenuous and repetitive instruction. Sparkle says, "It was a lot like teaching a class of three-year-olds in a way. You had to figure out ways to keep their attention, and make things fun, or you'd lose them."

The training formula they developed started to work. As the months went on, the skating improved exponentially, and a league started to emerge from what was originally more like an enthusiastic melee. The teams randomly birthed from local watering holes actually started to mean something when the skaters saw their dreams of staging a public bout gaining momentum.

In Dan's wake, the four captains had assumed the leadership of the league, adopting the cheeky moniker of "The She-E-Os." La Muerta, Anya (now Hot Lips Dolly), Nancy (Iron Maiden), and Heather Burdick (Sugar), who had replaced Amanda as captain of the Holy Rollers, served as the league's governing council, tasked with giving the group structure and direction.

The league was dubbed BGGW, or Bad Girl, Good Woman Productions. For a fee of $25 a month, skaters were entitled to admission to any league function and eight monthly practices. Most practices were held at the hangover hour of 8:00 AM on Saturdays, one of the few times the local rink was free. The fact that many BGGW members struggled to scare up the extra monthly expense before a bout was even scheduled, was a testament to their commitment. Their willingness to show up to practices at an ungodly hour on the weekends proved that they would to go to great lengths to make derby work.

But before the league could move to the next step—a public bout—there was one final thing they lacked: the rules of the game. Skaters ventured online to find any available explanation of how roller derby should be played. Questions that rollergirls are now asked routinely by novice fans—How do you score? How many blockers are there? What is a jammer?—were just as pressing back then to the BGGW players, whose knowledge of the game was limited to far distant memories of Saturday afternoons in front of the television as children.

Anyone who has tried to read a how-to guide on a sport knows how inscrutable the directions can appear in print form. Roller derby, a sport that had scarcely been seen live for the last decade, was definitely no exception. La Muerta notes that there was a time when the league was unclear as to whether the rules indicated two jammers *total*, or two jammers *per team*. Sparkle simply comments that the printed rules were "so freakin' vague" that they couldn't decipher much of anything. They may as well have been trying to learn jai alai from a Spanish-language guidebook.

It wasn't until they came across some old ESPN footage that the women understood the general gist of the game: three blockers and a pivot per team, who attempt to stop the one jammer for the opposing team from lapping them to score. From this, they were able to modify other sports drills to design effective lesson plans for training.

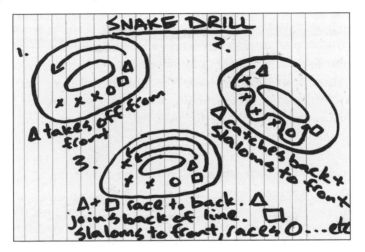

Sounds easy enough, right? Wrong. There were still plenty of details left to iron out. What was going to constitute a legal, versus an illegal, block? How long would the periods be? How should they determine the track dimensions? When would skaters serve their penalties? Would there be stopping between jams, or would the game be continuous?

Leagues today are fortunate to have manuals to answer all these difficult questions. But, back then, the women turned once again to roller derby's boyfriend—hockey—for some answers. And when the team-based contact drills of hockey failed, they would half-jokingly fall back on the sport's unofficial mantra: WWTHD?—"What would Tony Hawk do?"

In some notable cases, the skaters' ability dictated rules choices. In an older model of roller derby, each jam lasted for sixty seconds and jammers would thus have a one minute time limit to score points. In 2001, the skaters of the BGGW, try though they might, couldn't put many points on the board in that amount of time. "We weren't fast enough to score in sixty seconds," La Muerta admits, "So we changed the jam time to two minutes."

Little did they know it then, but that choice altered the sport forever. Those two-minute jams have endured to become the current standard in flat track derby.

Another modernization that the league implemented was what they dubbed "The Penalty Wheel." When a skater's on-track antics were off-track of the rules, the wheel would be spun to determine silly, fun, or embarrassing tasks for the skater to perform as a result. The "Mistress" of the BGGW wheel was an injured skater named Amber "Diva" Stinson. Diva would wrangle the crowd to help her lay the smackdown on the rule breaker. Penalties included a visit to "Spank Alley" (where select members of the crowd had the unique opportunity to tan a skater's hide), a fight with boxing gloves, or the ignominy of wearing the dreaded "Jackass Helmet."

PROFiLE: Spawna Chainsaw and Cherry Chainsaw

PHOTO BY SHARON LONG

PHOTO BY KERRY MCCLAIN

Olivia and Chloe Dansfiell are true pioneers of modern derby. Olivia, a.k.a. Cherry Chainsaw, was one of the original skaters with Bad Girl Good Woman Productions. Cherry was also the founding captain of the Texas Lonestar Roller Derby team called the Cherry Bombs. Her teenage daughter Chloe, a.k.a. Spawna Chainsaw, was one of the first girls to sign up for the Austin Derby Brats, the Texas Roller Girls Junior League.

If you were to analyze the Dansfiell family DNA, we're fairly certain you'd find derby embedded within their genetic code, along with plenty of badass.

Q: *Cherry, what are your earliest skate-related memories?*

CHERRY CHAINSAW: I skated a lot when I was younger. My parents didn't really have money for high-quality skates or to send me to lessons. But when I was six or seven, I'd be out there every day racing everybody in rentals and holding my own.

Q: *How did you get involved in derby?*

CC: I was friends with Anya (one of the original BGGW She-E-Os). She called me up and said, "Can you skate?" and I said, "Yeah." And she said, "You're on my team. By the way, practice is at six o'clock on Tuesday, be there!"

Q: *Spawna, back then you were just five years old. What was it like watching your mom play derby?*

SPAWNA CHAINSAW: I remember the first game that I went to; I wondered why they were all hitting each other. I kept wondering why they were doing that and if they were supposed to be doing that.

Q: *Because you had been taught hitting was wrong?*

SC: Yeah. It all seemed really strange to me.

Q: *Cherry, you definitely have a roller derby persona. How would you describe it?*

CC: I'd say loud. Belligerent. Sort of like a bull in a china shop.

Q: *And how does that differ from the real you, Olivia?*

CC: Not much at all.

Q: *You've won the "Most Feared" award three years running. How do you pull it off?*

CC: There's a mindset that I've always put on that helps. It's gonna sound really egotistical, but it's been helpful in the past, the mindset of "I'm better than you and

I'm just gonna mop the floor with you!"
When people see that, then they'll think twice
before coming up and tangling with me.

Q: Spawna, when did you decide to do derby?

SC: As I got older, about ten or eleven, I started to
understand better how they played and I thought it was really
cool. And I already knew how to skate. So when they started
doing a junior derby league last year in Austin, I signed up.

My younger sister is doing it, too. Her name is Hannah Monslamma.

**Q: You've got many years of skating ahead of you. What are your
goals for derby?**

SC: I'd really like to live up to my mom's name. I've got some pretty big
shoes to fill but I think I could do it. If I keep skating I feel I can achieve
her level of skill, but even faster.

Q: Cherry, what's it like watching your daughter do derby?

CC: It's exciting. But it's scary at the same time. My husband went to one
junior derby scrimmage and Spawna fell and rung her bell after landing on
her tailbone, which I taught her not to do! Anyway, it was a fluke thing . . .
But my husband's seen my injuries, my spills, my hobbling around for a week
before I go to the doctor, he's seen that and he knows that Spawna is just
like me and will be the same way.

Q: What effect has derby had on your relationship with your mom?

SC: Having a sport that both you and your mom do really helps with
your relationship. You get a lot closer and it gives you another
thing to talk about, and it's really fun compared to just going out
and doing other stuff. I'm glad that I have not just a mom-to-
daughter relationship, but a friend, too.

**Q: Cherry, do you think you'd ever face off against
Spawna on the track?**

CC: Oh God no! She'd kill me.

Given the amount of crowd interaction this would allow with the penalized skaters, it could take a firm hand to keep things civil. Any drunken yahoos in the crowd that got too friendly would have to face the wrath of Diva and her army of security. They were on task to make sure that a hand that groped a skater would soon be groping the exit.

LET'S RUMBLE!

On June 23, 2002, after a year and a half of grueling practices, the rowdy bar girls of Austin, Texas, had officially become athletes. It was the day of their first public bout, held at Skate World in Austin.

The Hellcats had their claws out to lasso the Rhinestone Cowgirls, while an impressively long line of bloodthirsty locals queued up in the parking lot. Adrenaline was high, and seeing the audience sent skaters' nerves into orbit—they were really doing this! Approximately 350 people vied to sit cross-legged on top of the rope lights that marked the outside edge of the track. The first whistle blew, beer was sloshed, cheers erupted, and the screech of wheels echoed off the mirror ball. The energy of the room turned the old sport back into a flesh-and-blood catfight that would have made Toughie and Gerry proud.

The bout was a contest full of heart. With a score shockingly low by today's three-digit norm, the Hellcats snatched the victory from the Rhinestones, forty-five to thirty-eight. And though the skaters fought viciously for victory on the track, the face-cracking smiles displayed by competitors and crowd alike were unmistakable—this was *fun*.

The Putas del Fuego and the Holy Rollers didn't have to wait long to have their shot at the glory. The second game followed two months later, on August 22 at Playland Skate Center. Would the BGGW be able to duplicate the success of the first game, or was it just a well-timed fluke? As the parking lot once again filled, this time with double the amount of ticket holders, the answer to each question became clear: Heck yes! And, hell no!

RHINESTONE COWGIRLS SHOW THEIR SPIRIT IN 2002

Austin, and the nation, were taking notice. Derby, it turned out, was a natural fit for the town, so proud of its "Keep Austin Weird" slogan. National and local media were attracted to the new sport, and a growing fan base was abuzz with anticipation for what BGGW would do next.

Unfortunately, BGGW was about to learn its first lesson in the difficulty of balancing the iron wills of its individual members with the more functional needs of a successful league. If anything can corrupt a utopian vision, of course, it's the green devil known as money.

BREAKING UP IS HARD TO DO

With a couple of successful games under their fishnets, the skaters realized they had created something that could have staying power. Growing ticket sales, media exposure, and skyrocketing self-confidence created differing views for the future of the league. A rift quickly grew between the She-E-Os and a large body of skaters as they regularly butted heads over league earnings and leadership.

Uncomfortable in her role as recruited, de-facto "Part-Owner," La Muerta ducked out of a situation that was rapidly growing as tense as a Friday on *Days of Our Lives*. This left Hot Lips Dolly, Iron Maiden, and Sugar to reconvene as the league's governing council. The three began to take steps to transform the league into a for-profit, registered business, where they would maintain most of the control as a result of their hard-working leadership positions.

But many of the skaters didn't like that plan. Citing their own hard work and years of contributions, they felt the ideal for the league would be a communal ownership, where every skater had a voice. The goal, in their eyes, was less about making money, and more about simply sustaining and promoting the sport they'd grown to love.

What started as casual gripes mentioned in passing during carpool rides to practice soon became nuclear grade philosophical fallout. Some were questioning how league funds were spent after a disastrous gamble on the production of a calendar. Then, on January 31, 2003, devastating news hit: beloved penalty mistress Amber "Diva" Stinson died of an overdose. Emotions reached a new precipice, only to be spurred further by the perceived mishandling of a major injury sustained by Lacy "Whiskey L'Amour" Attuso at an uninsured venue. The trifecta of malcontent was complete.

The majority of skaters called for a meeting to address the issues once and for all. Held around a bonfire at Cha Cha's house, anger between the conscientious objectors and the She-E-Os burned as hot as the flames that day. Shit, meet fan. What followed was an emotional divorce filled with a barrage of she said/she says that would rip the league in two.

As in any messy split, it's best not to attempt judging right and wrong from the outside. But, looking back, it's clear that what resulted from the skaters' parting of the ways would have an undeniable influence on the future of the sport.

PHOTO BY JAY LEE

A MINIATURIZED VIEW OF HOUSTON ROLLER DERBY

TWO TRACK TOWN

After differences between the coalition of upset skaters and the She-E-Os and their supporters were deemed irreconcilable, the small town of Austin suddenly found itself the breeding ground for two all-girl derby leagues. BGGW retained fifteen of the original skaters and set out to fulfill their dream of skating games on a traditional banked track under the new league moniker TXRD Lonestar Rollergirls. Sixty-five other skaters banded together to form the new, permanently flat track Texas Rollergirls.

As 2003 wore on, both leagues picked up the pieces and rolled forward. The Lonestar Rollergirls held tryouts that attracted skaters whose names would top their rosters for the next half decade. Veteran BGGW skaters Cherry Chainsaw, Hells Belle, Cha Cha, and Lunatic remained. They were soon joined by the fiery showstopper Chola, the phenomenal and aptly named Smarty Pants, and the mischievous Lux and her thousand-watt smile.

Meanwhile, the new Lonestar league bought a genuine vintage Bay Bombers banked track from its home in storage in Northern California.

In the heat of the Texas summer, the girls had a crash course in construction—banked tracks don't just pop out of the box ready for competition. With help from a former *RollerJam* skater out of Los Angeles, they got their first taste in puzzling together the behemoth banked track. And they would donate much blood, sweat, and bone to their baby over the next several years.

Once it was built, it was beautiful. The masonite sections fit together to create a kind-of tilted stage on which the girls could use physics to aid their momentum through the curves. Unlike the flat surface, where too much speed could often send you careening into the laps of happy spectators, the banked track curves provided gentle gravitational hugs, turning skaters into something akin to NASCAR racers.

But there was a catch: skating banked was also freakin' hard! For skaters who had just developed their track legs on the rink, the challenge of a tilted surface was enough to set them back a few strides. Strategy that may have worked wonders on the flat track was suddenly made moot by the appearance of the rail, or "fifth blocker," as it is sometimes called. Now, ending up out of bounds could mean an Icarus-like fall from a height of several feet to the unforgiving cement floor. Not to mention the introduction of ice packs to a whole different set of leg muscles!

While the Lonestars were exploring the joys of the third dimension, the Texas Rollergirls were gearing up for their first bout as an independent skater-owned-and-operated league. Though they made a concerted effort to distinguish themselves from the BGGW group by emphasizing the flat track aspect of their game, Sparkle notes they occasionally ended up being unwitting promoters of the crosstown league. "We were basically working for them, too," she recalls. "People would always ask about the old style banked track, and we'd find ourselves pointing out that there was another league in town that skated on one."

Also adding to the confusion was the fact that the Texas Rollergirls had retained three of the four original team themes. Along with the new, disco-themed Hustlers, the Texas Rollergirls consisted of the Hell Marys (Catholic schoolgirls), the Honkytonk Heartbreakers (cowgirls), and the Hot Rod Honeys (pin-up girls in black and pink).

While the residual hard feelings between the leagues surely made this contentious, it didn't seem to affect the popularity of the Texas Rollergirls. Their first bout, on July 20, 2003, broke the attendance records of any of the previous bouts skated with the BGGW.

A venue outside of town, and a less intimate environment, however, made the Lonestar Rollergirls' first outing slightly less successful. But, even with only a few hundred people in attendance, the match-up was not short on action. Cha Cha, a member of the Putas del Fuego, skidded on some track dust and was repaid with a leg break so gory it would make Dracula skittish.

Even with the setbacks, the Lonestar Rollergirls put on a scrappy, exciting game. Following their second public outing, they moved to a more deliciously illegal-looking and intimate warehouse that would provide a perfect edgy boost to the excitement for the rest of their season. Gradually that year, the She-E-Os each bowed out of leadership, leaving a new, fresh batch of girls to reform the league under a skater-owned-and-operated model similar to that of the Texas Rollergirls. And they, like their estranged flat track sisters, were headed for a run of success.

Upskating Members of the Community

SURE, WE'RE TOUGH AND mean on the outside, but spend time with any derby girl and you'll probably find she has a heart of gold and some causes she cares about deeply. Rollergirls like to give back to their community, and many leagues have used their time and talents to raise money for some wonderful charities.

PHOTO BY DOUGLAS "PAPA RAZZI" OTTO

MAD ROLLIN' DOLLS OF WISCONSIN CLEANING UP THE HIGHWAY

One tried and true method of fundraising is to hold a bout and donate proceeds to a worthwhile organization. For example, Arizona Roller Derby of Phoenix once sponsored a charity bout featuring the Hose Draggers, a firefighting-themed team, versus the Street Beaters, a team with a cop theme. The money they raised went to benefit the families of fallen firefighters and police officers.

Wasatch Roller Derby, a league in Salt Lake City, held a similar bout to help out the American Diabetes Association. For that game, a Carbo-Killers team took on the Sugar Slashers. The Tragic City Rollers of Birmingham, Alabama, once held a charity bout to help a five-year-old girl receive a heart transplant.

Of course, rollergirls have a lot of other talents besides skating that can be used for great causes. Skaters with the Terminal City Rollergirls of Vancouver, Canada rode their bikes to raise money for multiple sclerosis, and they held a sock drive for a women's shelter.

Giving back to the community isn't only beneficial in terms of good karma, it can also be a fantastic way to improve a league's public image. Seeing the same gals who beat each other up on roller skates wearing orange safety vests and picking up trash helps folks understand we aren't just hellions on wheels.

That's one of the reasons why the Mad Rollin' Dolls of Wisconsin adopted a local highway. "Ninety feet of track just wasn't enough," as they put it. "We're defending the country against litterbugs and making the roads safe and beautiful for hot rod mamas . . . well, Highway 51 anyway."

Being good Samaritans is also a great way to generate press. "A lot of radio stations, and some local newspapers and magazines, only want to promote us if it is for charity purposes," says Captain Morgan of the Long Island Roller Rebels. Among the worthwhile causes they've raised money for is a children's hospital that successfully saved the life of a skater's son by removing a tumor.

Many of the organizations leagues choose to support have some sort of personal connection. And in a sport where women dominate, it's little surprise that charities dealing with breast cancer are a popular choice. The Green Country Roller Girls of Tulsa, Oklahoma, found a genuinely creative way to raise money for women under the age of forty affected by breast cancer. They teamed up with Judi Grove, a breast cancer survivor who runs a project called Breast Impressions. Judi makes plaster casts of women's torsos (or "mammary memories," as she puts it). Prior to a game against the NWA Rollergirls of Arkansas, Judi made casts of skaters from both teams. The breast casts were decorated by local artists and auctioned off at the bout for a grand total of $2,700.

Judi says derby girls are a great fit for her work. "Since making the breast casts must be done bare-chested and roller derby women, for the most part, are not shy," she explains. "I also believe that women who are healthy, realize that their own health is at risk for breast cancer. That's one reason they feel strongly about raising awareness."

Not long after her trip to Tulsa, Judi started getting calls from other leagues. She's since worked with leagues throughout the U.S. and has raised more than $19,000. Judi's even earned her own derby name: Mammy O'Gram.

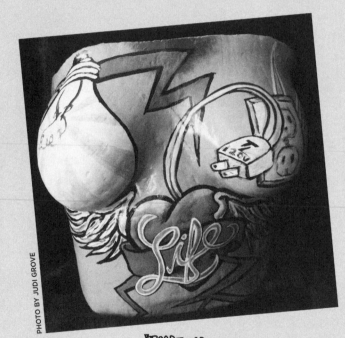

PHOTO BY JUDI GROVE

BREAST CAST OF JESSTER PHOT OF THE NORTHWEST ARKANSAS HILLBILLIES

The polarization of the original BGGW into the two Austin camps proved significant for the two paths that derby would follow up to the present day—banked and flat track play. Looking back on the split, one is reminded a bit of the band The Runaways. As a group they were terrific and talented, but inexperienced, and clearly pulling in different directions. When Lita Ford and Joan Jett went their separate ways, the world got a powerhouse of punk flash in Joan and a face-melting tower of balls-to-the-wall rock in Lita. Both styles would prove to be massive, and both would endure. In life and in derby, there's always room for variation.

meanwhile, in the rest of the country

LATE 2003 AND early 2004 proved to be a banner time for the revived sport of roller derby, as the tiny embers of the new derby movement began to burn bright in new locales. Little did we all know it, but across the country, the derby revolution was beginning to spread like a wonderful virus.

Allow your imagination to veer over the map slightly west of Austin and you might get a vision of a frustrated veteran of the punk rock scene in Phoenix. She's lying in bed, staring at a poster hanging above her feet. The poster advertises the classic derby exploitation film *Unholy Rollers*, and the gal is forming an idea. That woman is Denise Grimes, soon to become Ivanna S. Pankin.

Look even further west to Los Angeles, and you'd find two women working in a warehouse, building a dinosaur exhibition for Universal Studios Tokyo. One is covered in powder from a day of sculpting scenery, while the other is speckled in paint. The powdered one nearly drops her sandwich as the painted one glides by on roller skates during their lunch hour. A conversation develops between the two about a roller derby pipe dream. The sculptor is Rebecca Ninburg, who will hereafter be known as Demolicious. The painter is Wendy Templeton, the future Thora Zeen.

Far to the East in Brooklyn, professional sweater designer Karin Bruce hangs up her phone after an interesting conversation with her best friend, who just reintroduced herself as Thora. This roller derby thing they daydreamed about in college is happening, and Karin wants in. New York, meet Chassis Crass.

In the deep South, an unassuming but secretly outré thirty-one-year-old graphic designer named Laura Weakland in Raleigh, North Carolina, has just returned from a trip to Austin. Packed along with her souvenirs is a ticket stub from a Lonestar Rollergirls bout. With a voice still hoarse from screaming her head off in the stands, Laura pronounced herself Celia Fate, and set about recruiting like-minded women to bring derby to her backyard.

CELIA FATE CHAMPIONS ROLLER DERBY IN NORTH CAROLINA

PHOTO BY ABBY NARDO

Not since the near simultaneous invention of the corn dog at the Texas and Minnesota state fairs in the early 1940s has there been such a glorious confluence of delicious creations in the minds of strangers. In rapid succession, these five women in these four cities would pick up the derby virus from Texas and help to spread it like an epidemic over the next several years. And they didn't even know each other . . . yet.

Ivanna S. Pankin was the first out of the gate, when she posted ads in the Phoenix area asking if anyone wanted to join her roller derby league. At the time, she wasn't fully aware of what was going on in Texas, and set her mind to reinvent the polyurethane wheel. "Originally, we didn't think about where we would do it, that nobody knew how to skate, that we didn't have rules, that we didn't know how the game was played," she remembers. "I was just thinking of it in terms of a punk rock band. If we could get enough people, we'd figure it out."

Response to the ad was surprisingly strong, and before she knew what clotheslined her, Ivanna organized the hopefuls into a league christened Arizona Roller Derby, or AZRD. When one of her neighbors heard what was afoot, he offered to introduce her to a friend of his who was, much to her surprise, doing something similar in Austin. Little did she know that AZRD was not the first, but the third league to organize since the turn of the millennium.

A few months later, Demolicious and Thora Zeen were making the same discovery in Los Angeles—roller derby was alive and well in Texas. Better still, a couple of Lonestar Rollergirls were headed to L.A. to school them on it. This new league of Southern Californians had now been dubbed the L.A. Derby Dolls by original member Jenny Martinez, a.k.a. Juana Beatn'.

The visiting duo of Cha Cha (leg cast still intact) and Lunatic made Thelma and Louise look like Wally and the Beav. They arrived with Lonestar Rollergirls derby footage, ready to spread the love of the incubating sport—living proof that the Derby Dolls derby dreams could come true.

THE LA DERBY DOLLS ENJOY AN LA T-BIRDS GAME WITH TXRD LONESTAR ROLLER-GIRL CHA CHA

PHOTO COURTESY OF THE L.A. DERBY DOLL ARCHIVE

In November 2003, AZRD prepared for their first bout. Lonestar Rollergirls skaters Chola, La Loca, Suzy Homewrecker, and punk pixie Miss Conduct traveled to Phoenix to fill out gaps in Ivanna S. Pankin's team rosters. Like BGGW's first bouts, AZRD barely knew what to expect. Their skating skills were still germinal—undeveloped, but full of potential.

The L.A. Derby Dolls rented a van. Twenty passengers headed to Arizona to cheer on the action: thirteen were skaters, and seven were fifths of Jim Beam purchased at the state line. When they poured out of the van into their hostess's yard, Ivanna S. Pankin met the yin to her league's yang. The key elements of derby were staunchly present: the sober seriousness of heated competition and the extracurricular hedonism that came along with finding a gleeful group of enablers.

The skating itself may not have been the show of athletic prowess audiences have come to know today, but there was remarkable ambition. Only months before, derby was just another curiosity keeping Austin weird. But now, the derby nation was three cities strong. And all three were represented at one bout.

COURTESY DENISE GRIMES/IVANNA S. PANKIN

In Brooklyn, things were looking less promising for Chassis Crass. It was nearing winter in New York, frigid and forbidding. And despite its East Coast popularity in the early days, roller skating was a pastime much better suited to the pavements of Venice Beach than the urban labyrinth of the five boroughs.

A month before AZRD debuted to a sold out crowd, Chassis and her founding partner, a male friend named Lefty, invited a crowd of potential skaters to watch a copy of *Demon of the Derby*,

55

a documentary about Ann Calvello. Twenty people showed up, but according to Chassis, the crowd was comprised of "a lot of uninterested friends and boyfriends there for moral support." Only two women from that initial meeting, Baby Ruthless and Sybil Disobedience, would stick around long enough to skate in their first bout with Chassis a year later.

The next recruiting meeting in the spring was worse, with only two new people showing up. "And they were just random friends of our skater Margaret Thrasher, so we just got drunk and used the night as an excuse to talk more derby," Chassis remembers.

Recruitment efforts continued slowly, but help was on the way. With a word of introduction from Thora Zeen, Kasey Bomber elected to make a cross-country delegation of one, crashing on Chassis's couch and imparting her skating wisdom to the ragtag new Gotham Girls Roller Derby League in March 2004. Kasey happily shared everything she had learned on the west coast in her own four months of training with the dozen or so women who made up the initial Gotham Girls. It wasn't exactly the blind leading the blind, but considering that most of the women, including Chassis herself, hadn't yet seen a live bout, let alone skated in one, it was a much-needed exchange of information.

Meanwhile, in Raleigh, Celia Fate had spent the fall of 2003 researching roller derby for a North Carolina start-up. Her Austin friend, who had earlier introduced her to the sport, suggested that she check out the relative ease of starting a flat track league rather than wrangling the logistics of a banked track.

In her research, she discovered Ivanna's AZRD Yahoo group. "Instead of just spying on her, I decided to contact her," Celia recounts. "She was going through the same thing I was at the time, trying to recruit people." Ivanna's support and advice proved helpful, and both women benefited from the camaraderie and having someone with whom to share ideas.

According to Celia, "That whole fall, I was just trying to figure out how to make it happen. I was talking to local bars, and the people who *make* things happen around here." She partnered with a popular local watering hole and, like the Gotham Girls, hosted a derby movie night—though hers was more successful, with a solid group of interested girls coming out of the woodwork and hitching their skates to Celia's derby wagon.

The newly formed Carolina Rollergirls found a fortunate ally in local rink owner Sam Orr. "I think that Sam saw us as recruits for speed skating," Celia jokes. "He thought, 'Well, I'll teach you how to do that, and maybe you'll forget about this whole derby thing.'" Unfortunately for Orr, they stuck with derby. Nonetheless, he continued to champion the new league and provide them with a happy home base.

PACK FORMATION

By that spring, other leagues were brewing elsewhere. Tucson was taking notes from AZRD. Seattle mined the Texas Rollergirls for information vital to forming the Rat City Rollergirls. On the Missouri side of the Kansas City border, two coworkers at a local library gathered together the future 2007 national champs the Kansas City Roller Warriors.

Flat track derby was undoubtedly queen of the sport. This was roller derby that could be played at skating rinks, warehouses, parking lots, and high school gyms. The only materials needed to play are a roll of tape to mark the track and a sizeable flat surface—which made this style especially economical for the nation's new leagues. Skating on a banked track, rewarding as it later proved to be, created construction and permitting challenges, and flat track proved a hell of a lot easier to sell to potential venues and nervous insurance companies.

Even the L.A. Derby Dolls, determined to see fruition as a banked track contender, spent its first year learning the skills of the game with rigorous flat track training.

By May 2004, new alliances were starting to form among this latest crop of leagues. The Carolina Rollergirls traveled to Austin where the Texas Rollergirls showed them real life rock 'em–sock 'em roller derby. They watched a bout, then stayed for a week to train with these now-veteran skaters. Later in the week, the banked-track Lonestar Rollergirls gave the novices a taste of derby in 3-D.

That week, Carolina skater Harlot O'Scara suffered her league's first major injury when she tripped on the banked track and crushed her shoulder nearly beyond repair. Celia remembers the trip to the hospital where Harlot proved her rollergirl mettle, threatening to hit the doctor with her good arm if he touched her injured shoulder one more time. Floating on pain pills, wrapped and bound, Harlot nonetheless escaped the confines of the ER in time to cheer the first jam of the evening's Texas Rollergirls bout.

The following weekend, Austin unwittingly became the locus of a quasi derby summit. Chassis and Kasey planned to meet there to watch the Lonestar Rollergirls' Memorial Day weekend bout. Thanks to the wonders of MySpace communication, Kasey had convinced Celia to extend her derby tour as well. Kasey and Chassis were met by Celia, Chola, and a van load of Putas del Fuego armed with bout flyers and a party spirit. This was hospitality and bout promotion, Putas style. Scarcely were they off the plane before they were swept into the fold and conscripted into duty.

PHOTOS COURTESY OF KASEY BOMBER

When the Putas retired at a responsible eve-of-bout hour, General Lee Feisty and Ruby Sioux of the Rhinestone Cowgirls picked up the gauntlet of squiring around the now mostly inebriated visitors. They ferried Chassis and Kasey to a typical Austin house party where various members of the Texas Rollergirls were holding court. When they arrived in the yard, they were greeted by a tangle of legs and bursts of four-letter words, as beer soaked skaters Anna Mosity and Mean Streak barreled past in a friendly wrestling tussle. Electra Blu and Riff Scandell greeted them on the back porch. Any concern over tension between the opposing league skaters from Texas was quickly quelled with friendly welcomes and shared laughs.

HUDDLE

The diaspora of derby continued throughout the summer of 2004. The map became dotted with new upstart leagues. Texas Rollergirls' Lucille Brawl regaled her sister Colleen Bell with tantalizing tales from the track. She inspired her to found the Mad Rollin' Dolls in Madison, Wisconsin, where Colleen became Crackerjack. The Rat City Rollergirls motivated a sister league in Portland called the Rose City Rollers. Others followed, including the Rocky Mountain Rollergirls in Denver, the Bay Area Derby Girls in San Francisco/Oakland, the Minnesota Rollergirls in Minneapolis, and the Providence Rollergirls in Rhode Island.

Most leagues were finding that their success hinged on a few key things. They needed a handful of women with a lot of time to get things off the ground, and a locale with an enthusiastic fan base. But neither of these mattered if there wasn't a venue.

Take it from the Bay Area Derby Girls who faced a major real estate roadblock. "The closest rink was in San Ramon—a thirty to forty minute drive, and we were only allowed to skate open practices. We weren't even allowed to hit each other," Veronica "Killer Vee" LaRosa remembers with exasperation. Another venue, a roller hockey rink in Alameda, was not terribly interested in fostering roller derby. They allowed them to rent the space, but Killer Vee notes, "they would give us the shittiest times—10:30 PM to 12:30 AM on weeknights. For those of us who lived in the city, we didn't get home till 1:00 AM."

Finding venues was also an epic drama for the Windy City Rollers, skater Val Capone recalls. "There was nowhere to skate. They had just knocked down a giant roller rink called Rainbow Roller Rink where Led Zeppelin and Fugazi had played," she laments.

Windy City's first bouts were held in the old orchestra pit of the Congress Theater—a space that forced them to play on a track nearly half the regulation size, bordered on one side by a raised stage—a situation so dangerous that several leg breaks and a major case of whiplash made a move to the suburban rinks a no-brainer.

PHOTO BY MICHAEL COYOTE

GEORGIA O'GRIEF AND MISS FORTUNE OF THE RAT CITY ROLLERGIRLS
ENGAGE IN A BATTLE OF BALANCE

Unlike the Gotham Girls, the Windy City Rollers had no trouble recruiting despite cold weather and venue woes. Ninety-six hopefuls showed up at their first practice on September 22, 2004, and nearly all of them returned the following week, and the week after that, and so on.

As Windy City and other leagues began to grow, both the L.A. Derby Dolls and the Lonestar Rollergirls experienced unfriendly confrontations with law enforcement. Having parked their tracks in venues not strictly legal for public assembly, each saw seasons meet untimely changes of direction.

At one memorable bout, after a quarter of game play, the L.A. Derby Dolls were shut down by a legion of firemen sent by an anonymous tip to the fire marshal. Hundreds of rowdy fans started demanding their money back until fast-thinking announcer Evil E delivered an inspirational speech. "We hope you realize how hard these girls work. They all skate when they're tired, when they're hurt; they skate and train hours every week to put this league together, and they do it all for you . . ." Her speech did the trick and the crowd dispersed peacefully—with some even throwing in a couple of extra dollars. Few knew the words used to calm them down were the same ones originally delivered by Tom Hanks in the film *A League of Their Own.*

With a strong sense of community-building amongst the leagues through, and perhaps because of, these initial hardships, discussion soon began about uniting them under one banner. In the center of the action were the flat track pioneers, the Texas Rollergirls. The Texans hoped to not only continue distinguishing themselves from the Lonestar Rollergirls' banked track style of play, but also to foster a unified growth and promotion of the flat track version they championed. It didn't take much convincing to get the other teams on board.

The new collection of leagues, initially called the ULC—or United Leagues Coalition—would strive to create the template for a cohesive, nationwide version of the sport. To the dismay of some banked track skaters, the ULC's first rule was firm: Flat Track Only.

Alongside this new coalition, the impulse to organize a national conference was brewing. Keen to see their style of derby included in the fun, banked track skaters Chola and Kasey Bomber collaborated with Ivanna S. Pankin to devise a convention for flat and banked track skaters alike. In August 2005, Las Vegas played host to the first ever RollerCon, an all-inclusive national gathering.

Members from nearly all of the leagues existing at that time met in Sin City to scrimmage and talk shop over poolside cocktails.

It was, for most convention-goers, the first time they were able to skate with girls from across the country. Skaters from Dallas snagged whips from gals from Carolina. Both Austin leagues found themselves on the same track for the first time since their bitter split of 2003. Even veterans of the old school world of derby, Loretta "Little Iodine" Behrens and fiery manager Mizz Georgia Hase, were on hand to dish out tips and advice (Loretta dishing it on skates while clutching *a walker*). Each morning, girls with skates slung over their shoulders would pass by those still holding down the bar from the endless after-party of the night before.

For some of the RollerCon revelers, however, the trip was bittersweet. While en route to Vegas, the Big Easy Rollergirls from New Orleans had just, unknowingly, beat Hurricane Katrina out of town. Downed phone lines made their families unreachable, and none would learn the fate of their homes for days. Always keen to help sisters in need, many rollergirls offered up their couches and guest beds, while others busily coordinated efforts to replace clothes and belongings potentially lost to the tumult of the storm. For a time, the Big Easy girls found themselves to be a league without a town, but a team with its own nation of support.

Meeting fellow flat track purveyors at RollerCon fueled the desires of the United League Commission organizers. During the weekend of July 9, 2005, representatives from potential member leagues organized in Chicago. A standardized rule set for flat track derby was ratified over a series of headache-inducing pow-wows. A mission statement was created, outlining the requirements for membership in the association: only all-girl, flat track, skater-owned-and-operated leagues would qualify.

The ULC moniker was scrapped in favor of the more descriptive Women's Flat Track Derby Association or WFTDA (pronounced *wooft-dah* by insiders). Initially, twenty-two leagues were admitted, and officers were elected. Jennifer "Hydra" Wilson, a warm and friendly hydrologist from the Texas Rollergirls, was elected as the organization's founding president. Her first duty was to help organize the inaugural national derby tournament.

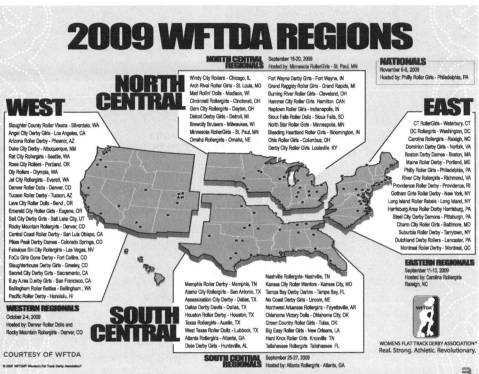

2009 WFTDA REGIONS

NORTH CENTRAL REGIONALS September 18-20, 2009
Hosted by: Minnesota RollerGirls - St. Paul, MN

NATIONALS
November 6-8, 2009
Hosted by: Philly Roller Girls - Philadelphia, PA

NORTH CENTRAL

Windy City Rollers - Chicago, IL
Arch Rival Roller Girls - St. Louis, MO
Mad Rollin' Dolls - Madison, WI
Cincinnati Rollergirls - Cincinnati, OH
Gem City Rollergirls - Dayton, OH
Detroit Derby Girls - Detroit, MI
Brewcity Bruisers - Milwaukee, WI
Minnesota RollerGirls - St. Paul, MN
Omaha Rollergirls - Omaha, NE

Fort Wayne Derby Girls - Fort Wayne, IN
Grand Raggidy Roller Girls - Grand Rapids, MI
Burning River Roller Girls - Cleveland, OH
Hammer City Roller Girls Hamilton CAN
Naptown Roller Girls - Indianapolis, IN
Sioux Falls Roller Dollz - Sioux Falls, SD
North Star Roller Girls - Minneapolis, MN
Bleeding Heartland Roller Girls - Bloomington, IN
Ohio Roller Girls - Columbus, OH
Derby City Roller Girls Louisville KY

WEST

Slaughter County Roller Vixens - Silverdale, WA
Angel City Derby Girls - Los Angeles, CA
Arizona Roller Derby - Phoenix, AZ
Duke City Derby - Albuquerque, NM
Rat City Rollergirls - Seattle, WA
Rose City Rollers - Portland, OR
Oly Rollers - Olympia, WA
Jet City Rollergirls - Everett, WA
Denver Roller Dolls - Denver, CO
Tucson Roller Derby - Tucson, AZ
Lava City Roller Dolls - Bend , OR
Emerald City Roller Girls - Eugene, OR
Salt City Derby Girls - Salt Lake City, UT
Rocky Mountain Rollergirls - Denver, CO
Central Coast Roller Derby - San Luis Obispo, CA
Pikes Peak Derby Dames - Colorado Springs, CO
Fabulous Sin City Rollergirls - Las Vegas, NV
FoCo Girls Gone Derby - Fort Collins, CO
Slaughterhouse Derby Girls - Greeley, CO
Sacred City Derby Girls - Sacramento, CA
B.ay A.rea D.erby Girls - San Francisco, CA
Bellingham Roller Bettles - Bellingham , WA
Pacific Roller Derby - Honolulu, HI

EAST

CT RollerGirls - Waterbury, CT
DC Rollergirls - Washington, DC
Carolina Rollergirls - Raleigh, NC
Dominion Derby Girls - Norfolk, VA
Boston Derby Dames - Boston, MA
Maine Roller Derby - Portland, ME
Philly Roller Girls - Philadelphia, PA
River City Rollergirls - Richmond, VA
Providence Roller Derby - Providence, RI
Gotham Girls Roller Derby - New York, NY
Long Island Roller Rebels - Long Island, NY
Harrisburg Area Roller Derby Harrisburg, PA
Steel City Derby Demons - Pittsburgh, PA
Charm City Roller Girls - Baltimore, MD
Suburbia Roller Derby - Tarrytown, NY
Dutchland Derby Rollers - Lancaster, PA
Montreal Roller Derby - Montreal, QC

EASTERN REGIONALS
September 11-13, 2009
Hosted by: Carolina Rollergirls
Raleigh, NC

WESTERN REGIONALS
October 2-4, 2009
Hosted by: Denver Roller Dolls and
Rocky Mountain Rollergirls - Denver, CO

SOUTH CENTRAL

Memphis Roller Derby - Memphis, TN
Alamo City Rollergirls - San Antonio, TX
Assassination City Derby - Dallas, TX
Dallas Derby Devils - Dallas, TX
Houston Roller Derby - Houston, TX
Texas Rollergirls - Austin, TX
West Texas Roller Dollz - Lubbock, TX
Atlanta Rollergirls - Atlanta, GA
Dixie Derby Girls - Huntsville, AL

Nashville Rollergirls- Nashville, TN
Kansas City Roller Warriors - Kansas City, MO
Tampa Bay Derby Darlins - Tampa Bay, FL
No Coast Derby Girls - Lincoln, NE
Northwest Arkansas Rollergirls - Fayetteville, AR
Oklahoma Victory Dolls - Oklahoma City, OK
Green Country Roller Girls - Tulsa, OK
Big Easy Roller Girls - New Orleans, LA
Hard Knox Roller Girls - Knoxville TN
Tallahassee Rollergirls Tallahassee FL

WOMENS FLAT TRACK DERBY ASSOCIATION®
Real. Strong. Athletic. Revolutionary.

SOUTH CENTRAL REGIONALS September 25-27, 2009
Hosted by: Atlanta Rollergirls - Atlanta, GA

COURTESY OF WFTDA
© 2009 WFTDA® Women's Flat Track Derby Association®

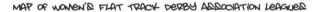

MAP OF WOMEN'S FLAT TRACK DERBY ASSOCIATION LEAGUES

THE BOOM

The charter members of WFTDA were all skating in the United States . . . but the gospel of roller derby was already being spread in far corners of the globe.

In 2005, Toronto and Edmonton started leagues in Canada. Meanwhile, fräuleins in Germany's Stuttgart Valley and skaters from London, England, did the same. Challenges for the European leagues were especially unique, since roller derby had always been a primarily American pastime. Audiences and potential skaters alike were baffled by the game—which most of their countrymen had never heard of, let alone seen. Nonetheless, the founders of the leagues persisted, and by 2006 they were joined by leagues in New Zealand and Australia, making the sport truly international.

PROFiLE: Hydra

Every burgeoning democratic nation needs an inaugural leader; someone who is brave enough to take responsibility for mistakes, patient enough to foster a work in progress, and generous enough to give themselves to the nation's citizens. The United States had George Washington.

The WFTDA had Jennifer Wilson, a.k.a.
Hydra. Hydra is a former collegiate handball
champion who began her derby career at the
genesis of the modern movement in Austin. But
when her derby democracy called for leadership, she
gave up some of her treasured time as a Texas Rollergirl all-
star to help give structure to the sport she'd helped create.

Q: *When did you start skating derby?*

HYDRA: I joined BGGW in November 2001, after attending tryouts
and being one of the few people there who knew how to skate.
Strangely enough, I showed up to tryouts in a pink and black miniskirt
ensemble. I thought it was pretty slutty and totally inappropriate for
such a rough sport like roller derby, but it was exactly what they were
looking for! So, I was already in roller derby when my current league,
the Texas Rollergirls, formed in the spring of 2003. I decided to go with
the Texas Rollergirls instead of staying with my old league, Bad Girl, Good
Woman (BGGW).

Q: *What initially attracted you to derby, since there weren't exactly
any models for comparison at the time?*

H: The only reason I even showed up at the BGGW tryouts was to spite the
girl who snubbed me with the tryouts flyers. The night before, I was at a
bar with my friends. One of the BGGW girls came up to us with a stack
of flyers in her hand. She was doing outreach for the tryouts the next
morning. She gave a flyer to my friend and I stuck out my hand for
one. She looked me up and down, deemed me unworthy, and turned
around and walked off without giving me a flyer. I ripped the paper
out of my friend's hand—I read it and said, "I'm going to those
tryouts. Fuck that bitch." The next morning at eight, I dragged
myself out of bed and went to the rink, still drunk, still in my
black miniskirt and pink Circle Jerks concert t-shirt. I put
on rental skates and hit the floor. I got an eye roll from
that flyer snob, but the captain of the Hellcats loved

my skills and style and drafted me to the team right then and there.

Q: *Once you were involved, did you always see the sport as something that would blow up to global proportions?*

H: Back in the early 2000s, I never thought it would get this big—we were too disorganized and there was so much to figure out about playing the game and how to pull off events. I figured a few other cities would pick up roller derby over time, but I thought it would only be the big cities with a good scene. I am totally and pleasantly surprised to see it doing so well everywhere.

Q: *What were some of the challenges of being the first to hold the position of WFTDA president?*

H: The biggest challenge was the huge workload, because I was one of the few people who knew what was going on in all areas of the organization. Even to this day, the organization is large, volunteer-run, and has a lot of turnover, and that makes it very difficult to keep everyone on the same page with our policies and the big picture. A final challenge that I think will always be part of the organization is figuring out the direction that the members want the organization to go in the future. Survey results and meetings show that people's ideas are all over the map. One group wants the WFTDA to drop the "W" and "FT" parts of our name and be an all-inclusive organization, while another group wants the WFTDA to be even stricter on our membership policies. It's the same situation in almost every sector of the association and impossible to find a direction that satisfies everyone.

Q: *Looking back from this point in derby's development to the first year or so of your experience with the Texas Rollergirls is there anything from the early days that you miss that you feel may have fallen victim to the sport's evolution?*

H: I think that a common perception is that the fun and silliness has been sucked out of the game since taking it to a nationally competitive level. But, everyone has to realize that this is not a simple game of tic-tac-toe—this is a full-contact sport on wheels and it needs to be taken seriously. I'm one of the biggest fans of high-level play—I scream myself hoarse after just one day at Nationals! I'm positive that there are many skaters out there today who truly enjoy skating at this excelled level. Plus, it doesn't have to be that way (megaserious)—you can still have fun playing derby, either on your home team or on a recreational league. You don't have to take it to the top if you don't want to be that serious.

Q: How the heck does it feel to have the WFTDA Nationals trophy named after you?

H: It's so cool! I hope to go to every Nationals from here on out to see how my trophy is doing . . . give her a little spit shine and a kiss on the heel. At the same time, it can be embarrassing when people talk about it too much. I'm rather shy or modest, or whatever it is, about too much direct attention on me. The WFTDA totally surprised me on that one and made me cry like a little girl!

MEANWHILE, IN THE REST OF THE COUNTRY

67

PROFILE: Polly Purgatory

PHOTO BY DENISE KAUFMANN

Historically, roller derby has been a primarily American pastime. But in the past few years, groups of tenacious women across the pond have been striving to translate the sport into every language. One of those women is Marta Popowska, a.k.a. Polly Purgatory, a grad student at Stuttgart University. In 2006, Polly founded the Stuttgart Valley Rollergirls in Germany. Derby in Deutschland? Wunderbar!

Q: Was it difficult to find girls to join the league?

POLLY PURGATORY: Yes, it was, and it still is due to the fact that we are the very first roller derby league in Germany. But we have a little bonus of being kind of exotic, so we receive a lot of publicity through press and TV. The sport is getting more popular, and with increasing fame, more girls want to join.

Q: What do you think holds girls back from joining?

PP: I think a lot of girls like the sport but are too intimidated to get in touch, at first. When they see us play or they see all these crazy-looking, tattooed girls, they think they have to be that way as well—even though 50 percent of us are quite "normal" looking. But we try to make it clear that we are looking for dedicated new girls from all kinds of backgrounds and lifestyles to join.

Q: Being so isolated from other leagues, how did you approach your training?

PP: Nowadays, barely anyone in Germany does quad skating, and it never was as famous as in the U.S. But we knew a former street skater who taught us to skate technically well (I hope) and one of our first girls was American and used to skate as a kid and was quite dedicated. Our girls Dolly BustHer, Evil Lynn, and Titty Twista came to be great coaches after a while. We get a lot of input from Internet forums too, of course.

Q: How did you manage to teach people in Stuttgart Valley about roller derby, given that they'd never seen it before?

PP: That was a tough thing. You wouldn't believe how often people asked "And where is the ball??" because they only knew the stupid movie *Rollerball!* You have to imagine that Europe never had roller derby, and most people thought we were tattooed chicks in miniskirts just skating in a circle until they saw a bout. Most people didn't believe it was a real sport. That was annoying. But they changed their opinion after they watched their first bout.

Q: How are your crowds?

PP: People love it here. In Stuttgart we have a bout every three or four months, and it is sold out every time with about 500 to 650 people attending. We are looking for a bigger venue at the moment.

Q: What are your hopes for your league in the future?

PP: I hope that our league will grow constantly. I really hope for more German leagues to crop up so that we can bout more in Germany. Flying over to Great Britain [where their closest competitors are located] or organizing international events is expensive and exhausting, although we like to do this kind of travel from time to time.

Q: So, are all your skate names in English, or do you have any really good ones in German that you'd like to share and explain for our readers?

PP: Almost all skate names are in English. But we have a few funny German ones. One girl is named Isolde Maduschen. Isolde is an old fashioned German name. "Maduschen" also means something like "I should take a shower" in Swabian dialect. Sounds very funny in German.

In 2006, roller derby also made it to television once again, this time in the form of a reality show on the A&E network called *Rollergirls*. The show followed the lives of TXRD Lonestar Rollergirls such as Punky Bruiser, Miss Conduct, Lux, and Cha Cha.

A&E thought they had a surefire hit. After all, rollergirls are sexy and have fantastic, one-of-a-kind personalities. The inevitable bickering that arises within a league (a.k.a. "derby drama") was just the sort of thing reality TV watchers relish. To top it all off, each episode ended with footage from an actual TXRD bout. Unfortunately, the show itself met with little success. Though it had a small loyal following, the ratings for *Rollergirls* were weak. The program was cancelled before the last episodes of the season even aired. But while the show may not have inspired big ratings, its effect on the sport itself was huge.

In derby country, we have a designation: there are B.R.G. leagues, and there are A.R.G. leagues–Before-*Rollergirls* and After-*Rollergirls*. In 2006, the number of leagues in the world had nearly tripled from the 2005 tally and the numbers have grown by at least one hundred leagues a year since.

Derby Domination:
League Expansion Since 2001*

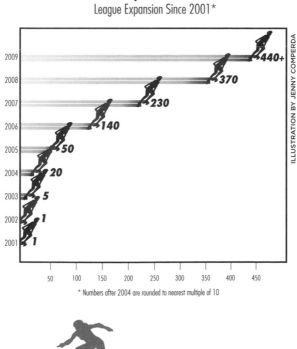

ILLUSTRATION BY JENNY COMPERDA

2009	440+
2008	370
2007	230
2006	140
2005	50
2004	20
2003	5
2002	1
2001	1

50 100 150 200 250 300 350 400 450

* Numbers after 2004 are rounded to nearest multiple of 10

EIGHT WHEELED EXPLOSION

Which brings us to . . . now.

Derby has come a long way since the BGGW women first laced up their skates. What was once the pipe dream of a quasi-con man in Austin continues to grow and spread through the diligence and constant work of leagues around the world. To write about all that has happened so far would take several volumes—with each league likely having their own tome to contribute to the canon.

These are merely the first chapters of an ever-evolving history, a history that grows each day. This is simply our attempt to record the origins before they break up in the fuzzy reception of oral history's telephone game.

In the end, some questions remain: Why derby? Why now? What was in the air in 2003 that made all of these strangers sit up and come to attention? Was it simply that we were a generation of twenty- and thirty-something women raised on those idyllic childhood derby memories that so inspired the original BGGW crew? Or was it that we were that generation living through a new era for women? Many of us already had careers, friends and families. We had accomplished so much, but we were still hungering for something more.

Sparkle Plenty, now retired, is thoughtful about the sport's attraction. "I think girls across the world were looking for something non-traditional," she opines. "Not just scrapbooking." And perhaps it is as simple as that—for all the twenty-first century technology and constant digital contact, women were still bored by the status quo and looking for something different, yet simple and human.

Roller derby also welcomed everyone, regardless of their athletic ability. Countless women who had failed miserably at traditional sports were amazed at what they could physically achieve when surrounded by supportive eight-wheeled colleagues. Derby also provided a rare outlet, an opportunity for women no matter what their size and shape to feel sexy. As our alter egos, it was okay to show a little more skin.

Regardless of reasons why, the fact remains that derby is spreading, growing, and succeeding beyond the wildest imagination of the women who laid the groundwork.

In fact, as these words are being typed, there are girls out there somewhere, trying derby names on for size, headed to their brand new league's very first practice. And from the wheels of our worn-out skates, to the tip of our battered helmets, we say, "Welcome, and roll on!"

TIME OUT! *Advanced Derby Geography*

GET OUT YOUR PENCILS, derby scholars. Class is in session. Sure, even those whose helmets are a holdover from their days on the short bus can tell you that Tucson Roller Derby is located in Tucson and the London Rollergirls hail from London, England. But some leagues are subtler with their name choices and tap into their hometown's culture or history. See if you can decode the secret language of derby geography by matching the name of the league with its correct location.

RADIOACTIVE ROLLER GIRLS	Baton Rouge, Louisiana
SLAUGHTERHOUSE DERBY GIRLS	Cleveland, Ohio
RED STICK ROLLER DERBY	Seattle, Washington
CHARM CITY ROLLER GIRLS	Paducah, Kentucky
QUEEN CITY ROLLER GIRLS	Albuquerque, New Mexico
AULD REEKIE ROLLER GIRLS	Buffalo, New York
BURNING RIVER ROLLER GIRLS	Greeley, Colorado
DUKE CITY DERBY	Birmingham, Alabama
TRAGIC CITY ROLLERS	Edinburgh, Scotland
RAT CITY ROLLERGIRLS	Baltimore, Maryland

1. **Radioactive City Roller Girls:** This league is located in **Paducah, Kentucky**, home of the Paducah Gaseous Diffusion Plant, the only operating uranium enrichment facility in the United States. It's great for a town to have a unique industry, but most prefer one that doesn't get investigated for the improper disposal of radioactive waste into their soil, landfills, and ground water, as this plant did in 1999.

2. **Slaughterhouse Derby Girls: Greeley, Colorado**, where this league hangs their helmets, is also a city of industry. That industry is meat. You might recognize the town from reading *Fast Food Nation*, which cites the area as one of the primary meatpacking locales for the U.S. fast food industry. Next time you bite down on a burger, you might just be wrapping your lips around a little bit of Greeley.

3. **Red Stick Roller Derby:** This moniker belongs to our Cajun cousins down in **Baton Rouge, Louisiana**. If you're a survivor of French 101, you might have already guessed—Baton Rouge is "red stick" *en français*! The city was so named in 1699 by French explorer Sieur d'Iberville after spotting a reddish cypress pole covered by bloody fish and animals that marked the boundary between the Houme and Bayou Goula tribal hunting grounds on the Mississippi River.

4. **Charm City Roller Girls:** To many of us, **Baltimore, Maryland**, is best known as the home of John Waters—not exactly the purveyor of grace and charm. But, back in 1974, in an attempt to draw visitors to this great city, adman Bill Evans devised a plan. Tourists could obtain an empty charm bracelet at one of the local visitor's centers and then collect a different charm for every official tourist attraction they patronized. The promotion disappeared like Ricki Lake's career, but the nickname "Charm City" stuck around.

5. **Queen City Roller Girls:** In the state of New York, New York City is king. But every great king needs a queen, and for NY, that queen is **Buffalo**. This league pays homage to its hometown's ranking as second most populous city in the state.

6. **Auld Reekie Roller Girls:** We travel overseas to **Edinburgh, Scotland**, to decode the mystery of this league's name. Auld Reekie is Scots for "old smoky." Edinburgh kept this nickname from the days when buildings were heated by coal and wood fires, and the air was filled with impenetrable columns of smoke from the ubiquitous chimneys.

7. **Burning River Roller Girls:** Have you ever seen water catch fire? Well, the residents of **Cleveland, Ohio**, have. On June 22, 1969, residents were surprised to look out their windows and see a five story blaze ripping across the highly polluted, oil-contaminated water of the Cuyahoga River. Though a dubious event the city would like to forget, the Burning River Roller Girls wear it like a badge.

8. **Duke City Derby:** No doubt this league saw the benefits of relying on their city's nickname, if for no other reason than it is easier to spell than Albuquerque! Back in the sixteenth century, **Albuquerque, New Mexico**, was a hotbed of trading posts for Western travelers, and those still searching in vain for the fabled lost Cities of Gold. In the early 1700s, business was comparatively booming, so the governor of the area officially established the city, naming it after Spaniard Francisco Fernandez de la Cueva, the Duke of Alburquerque. The city later dropped the extra "r" in the moniker.

9. **Tragic City Rollers: Birmingham, Alabama**, is this league's hometown. Originally dubbed "Magic City" when it was created after the Civil War to draw Northern

industry to the South, a subsequent history of civil and racial unrest forever altered the name. On September 15, 1963, Ku Klux Klan member Robert Chambliss bombed the Sixteenth Street Baptist Church, a regular meeting spot for Civil Rights leaders. The four African American children killed in the blast became known as the Birmingham Four, and set off widespread protests that galvanized the Civil Rights movement.

10. **Rat City Rollergirls:** There was a time when "Rat City" was a slur on **Seattle, Washington**. Legend has it that rodents were once prevalent in the streets of a low-income neighborhood known as White Center. The name may also be a nod to the "rink rats" who roller skated at the still-operating Southgate Skate Center. Regardless of the name's origin, the RCRG has assuredly co-opted the city's former insult and given it the flavor of pride.

6

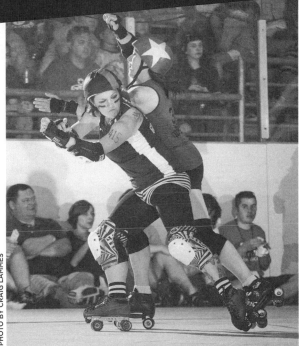

PHOTO BY CRAIG LAMMES

JOY COLLISION LIVES UP TO HER NAME BY SHUTTING DOWN LADY QUEBEAUM IN A CHARM CITY HOME GAME

SO HOW THE hell do you play roller derby?

For decades, the basics of roller derby have remained pretty much intact; the universal premise being that the jammer has to make it through the pack once and after that, every time she passes a skater on the opposing team, she earns a point.

77

Beyond that, the rules have evolved tremendously, especially during the twenty-first century renaissance of roller derby. That's one of the benefits of being a D.I.Y. sport—we get to make our own laws!

Just as high school, college, and Major League Baseball have different rules for the same basic game, you'll find different sets within modern roller derby, as well. There are rules created by individual banked and flat track leagues; edicts devised by various derby associations that include multiple leagues; and ordinances developed especially for tournaments or other special occasions.

Rules in roller derby are important. We rely on them to try and keep the game fair and safe (well, as safe as can be in a violent, full-contact sport).

Derby rules can also be incredibly obtuse and a tad crazy-making to those who just want to skate fast and hit hard. For example, take a look at 3.5.10.1 of the Women's Flat Track Derby Association's rules, version 4.0:

> If, in a given jam, the Jammer who received a star pass (formerly the Pivot) is sent to the penalty box, she remains her team's Jammer when her penalty spans into the next jam. A different player is permitted to play as Pivot in the next jam.

If reading that brought on waves of apoplectic confusion you haven't felt since that AP Calculus class you failed—don't panic, we're here to help. Welcome to Derby 101.

DERBY DEFINITIONS

Let's start with the lexicon. Modern roller derby is filled with plenty of odd terminology—expressions like "sin bin" and "pivot panty" might sound like props on a porn set, but they're actually phrases heard frequently on the track. Die-hards who want to be fluent in lingua-derby can geek out and hit up derby websites like fracturemag.com, fiveonfivemag.com and bloodandthunder-mag.com. The rest of you should be able to get by with the following key terms:

JAMMER—A jammer is a skater able to score for her team. Jammers tend to be the swiftest, most agile skaters on the team. They're also often the crowd favorites since they're the ones who score points.

PHOTO BY JOE SCHWARTZ WITH SPECIAL THANKS TO THE PHILLY ROLLERGIRLS, A NON-PROFIT ORGANIZATION, AND TO THE EAST COAST DERBY EXTRAVAGANZA—WWW.PHILLYROLLERGIRLS.COM

A LITTLE JAMMER LOVE BETWEEN A MADISON DAIRYLAND DOLL AND A TAMPA BAY DERBY DARLIN

BLOCKER—A blocker is a skater who tries to block or prevent the jammer from the opposite team from scoring. A blocker also tries to help *her own* team's jammer score. Larger skaters often wind up being blockers as they can deliver big, terrifying hits. That said, there are some Amazonian gals who make great jammers and some tiny but terrifying blockers weighing in at less than one hundred pounds. Great blockers are so scary they make other skaters cower just by looking at them.

RULES OF THE GAME

79

PIVOT—A pivot is a special type of blocker. The pivot's role is to control the speed of the pack. Often found in the front, the pivot is like a puppet master controlling the ever-moving morass of skaters. In rare instances, the pivot can become the jammer in a play called "passing the star." We'll get to that in a bit.

PACK—The pack is comprised of the blockers and pivots from both teams skating in a given jam. The pack should move fast and furiously—with skaters rotating positions. A novice pack may look like a bunch of nervous seventh-graders at a dance—wanting to make physical contact, but desperately afraid. A pack of expert skaters, on the other hand, will be hitting each other constantly, making *Faces of Death* look like a Doris Day musical. Because of the skaters' close proximity to each other within a pack, when one person falls, it can create a domino effect with skates and limbs flying in all directions.

PERIODS OF PLAY

A game of roller derby is usually referred to as a **bout**. According to the Women's Flat Track Derby Association's rules, a bout is sixty minutes of play, divided into two periods lasting a half hour, with a break in between. Usually a banked track derby bout is also an hour of play, divided into four quarters that are each fifteen minutes long.

No matter which style of derby is being played, the action is made up of short periods of play called **jams**. These jams are races in which the two teams compete to score points. In flat track derby, a jam lasts a maximum of two minutes. In banked track derby, a jam lasts no more than one minute.

WHAT HAPPENS DURING A JAM

At the beginning of each jam, both teams send a group of skaters up to the track and they form a pack. The pack includes a pivot from each team, marked with a cloth cover worn over their helmets with a stripe running down the middle. These helmet covers are affectionately known as **pivot panties.**

In addition to the pivots, the pack consists of an additional three blockers from each team (sometimes fewer if there is a penalty from the previous jam). Blockers' helmets go commando, or panty-free.

A jammer from each team lines up several feet behind the pack. The jammers wear **jammer panties** with stars on both sides on their helmets.

After some scuffling for position and perhaps a bit of good-natured trash talk, the jam begins when the referee blows the whistle once. This signals the pack to take off skating around the track in a counterclockwise direction. Shortly after that, the referee blows the whistle again—this time with two short blasts. That signals the two jammers to begin racing in the same direction as the pack.

When the jammers take off, they skate up to the pack and then try to skate through it with minimal bodily damage. Blockers will do just about anything they can to stop the jammer from the opposite team. They'll distract her, skate in front of her, hip-check her; they'll even turn around and slam her to the ground if rules for that bout permit.

Jammers will do almost anything they can to avoid these hits, like a running back dashing around the other team to make a touchdown. A great jammer is an agile skater who will quickly slink around blockers and leap over fallen skaters. When she does get knocked down, she'll bounce back on her skates in the blink of an eye.

When a jammer makes it out of the pack first, she becomes what's known as the **lead jammer**, a strategically important role, as will be explained below. Once a jammer manages to roll with the hits and fight her way through the pack the first time, she skates as fast as she can until she catches up with the pack for a second time. Now, every time she passes a skater from the other team, she earns a point.

Jammers can't earn more than one point from an opposing teammate unless they go all the way through the pack, and pass them once again. When a jammer completely laps the opposing jammer, she'll earn an additional point, known as a **grand slam**, each time she passes her again.

Usually, most of the hitting in derby comes from blockers and pivots, but jammers are allowed to get physical, too. A jammer may decide to pass a blocker by knocking her on her ass. Or she might throw a hip at her rival jammer as a way to prevent her from scoring first.

A jam comes to an end when the jam clock runs out of time and is signaled by the ref with a series of whistle blasts. The lead jammer also has the special privilege of **calling off the jam**, if she so chooses. She signals this by placing her hands on her hips and does so to prevent the other jammer from scoring points. Jammers often call off the jam with great flair, drawing thunderous crowd approval for their victory!

TEXAS ROLLERGIRLS' TEXECU-
TIONER CAT TASTROPHE CALLS
OFF THE JAM

PROFILE: Kamikaze Kim

Several times in this book, you've read that roller derby is a sport for all shapes and sizes. Kim Saito, a.k.a. Kamikaze Kim of the Rat City Rollergirls in Seattle, Washington, is a little more than five feet of proof. Though she may be small in stature, one glimpse at her biceps (tattooed with the slogan GUN SHOW), and you'll know she packs a huge wallop. As a member of Team Awesome and one of the skaters who helped lead her former league, then-seventeenth-ranked Duke City Derby Girls of Albuquerque, New Mexico, to the 2008 WFTDA nationals, Kim will be the first to tell you that in derby, you should never count out the underdog.

Q: When people think about derby, they usually think skaters are all giant Amazons—but badass comes in all sizes. What would you say are some advantages in this sport of being somewhat smaller?

DOWN AND DERBY

KAMIKAZE KIM: Generally, smaller stature skaters tend to be faster and more agile. Although I've seen my share of bigger girls that are just as fast and agile.

Q: Do you feel that you are ever underestimated because of your size? I'm guessing that doesn't last too long . . .

KK: Hmmm. I don't know. I always feel like I have a target on my back. But that could just be the usual jammer paranoia.

Q: Will you tell us the story behind the Gun Show tattoos?

KK: Hahaha! Well, I had the idea for a while but never really did anything about it. Then one year I decided it would be my "Year of Fun" to make up for the year prior, which had been a pretty shitty one for me, personally. And what is more fun than tattoos? Mostly I did it because it's hilarious! I was starting to take myself way too seriously and felt that I needed to lighten up. And so what if I'll have these when I'm eighty? I'll be the beefiest eighty-year-old ever! Plus, all the ladies seem to like them . . . a lot!

Q: Do you find that there is a community feel with Asian skaters throughout derby?

KK: When I started four years ago, I didn't see a lot of Asian skaters. Today, there are so many leagues across the country and more and more skaters from all racial backgrounds are playing derby. At the 2009 East Coast Extravaganza in Philly, I was lucky to be a part of the formation of the very first all Asian team, Rice. We played against Beans, a Mexican team. (Rice took the win, because we are the superior race. Ha, ha!) It was so much fun not only because it was the first ever Asian team, but because there were so many amazing skaters on the roster. Plus, we have the best strategy, because no one can tell any of us apart.

But, to answer your question, I do feel a sense of community skating with other Asian skaters. I wish I could do it more. I also love that we can all joke about our Asian-ness with each other. We formed this team because we already dominate the classical music field, math, science, extreme eating, grocery stores, and laundromats. So what's left? Derby! We're such overachievers.

Q: Can you tell us a bit about Duke City's road to the Nationals in 2008?

KK: Well it was an incredible journey. That year started out pretty bad. We lost our venue and half the league quit. Those that were left thought about leaving to other leagues. But we decided to make the most of what we had. So the only functioning team in Duke City was our travel team, the Munecas Muertas. We didn't even have a season scheduled and just picked up games throughout the year. When we got to Western Regionals, we had only played a total of three games that season. In the second round we faced the Kansas City Roller Warriors (KCRW), who at the time were defending 2007 National Champions and ranked #1 in the nation (we were ranked seventeenth). When we beat them, we automatically qualified for Nationals. It was totally incomprehensible. We could not believe it. That win also thrust us into the national spotlight, which we were not accustomed to. Once we got to Nationals it was just a total whirlwind. Playing Gotham was amazing and despite the loss, we learned a lot in the process. It was such an honor to be sharing the track with such amazing teams. It was truly an unforgettable experience.

Q: What would you say is your favorite derby moment so far?

KK: Favorite skating moment would have to be that win at Regionals against KCRW. Not just because it qualified us to go to Nationals, but because KC is such a great team to play and both teams fought hard until the final whistle. Also, being a part of Team Awesome and KC/DC (mixed Kansas City/Duke City ad hoc banked track team). Both were great games and are some of my fondest derby memories.

As far as non-skating moment, since we were discussing Asian skaters earlier . . . At 2008's Nationals, Duke City skated in the game that just followed the Texas versus Carolina game. I was sitting on our bench before our game and this guy from the audience comes up to me and says to me, "Rice Rocket, you're amazing!" So I looked at him and said, "Thanks." I didn't have the heart to tell him that I wasn't Rice Rocket (she was on the Texas Rollergirls). Any time I get confused for Rice Rocket is a good day! That is real!

PHOTO BY KERRY MCCLAIN

BREAKS, HALF-TIMES AND END OF BOUT

In a given period of play, jams continue with brief breaks in between each jam. Half-times usually last about a half hour, and will usually feature some sort of entertainment. This could include performances by bands, drill teams, or belly dancers. Oklahoma City Roller Derby has even featured extreme animal shows at half-time, complete with snakes and kangaroos.

Some leagues like to get the audience involved during half-time. That might mean holding mini-scavenger hunts, donut-eating contests, or letting kids race around the derby track on Big Wheels. Half-times are also a great opportunity for running raffles to help a league earn extra money. Of course these breaks also give skaters time to get some rest, freshen up, and revise their team strategies. When skating resumes, jams will continue until the game clock runs out of time. At that point, whichever team has the most points wins.

WHAT ABOUT TIES?

Every now and then, the game clock hits zero and both teams have the same amount of points. In most flat track derby bouts, a tie score results in an overtime jam. But this jam is special for two reasons: 1) unlike a regular jam, it can't be called off by the lead jammer, and 2) the jammers start earning points on their *first* pass through the pack. If the score remains tied after one overtime jam, then another one will be held . . . and another . . . and another . . . until one team has more points than the other.

In most banked track derby bouts, tie scores result in what's known as a "sudden death" jam. Points are not scored until the second pass through the pack, but whichever team scores the first point automatically wins the bout.

TIME OUT!

Tournaments

AFTER ALL THE HARD work you put in at practices, meetings, and volunteer obligations, it is the action of the bout that reminds you all that effort comes with an awesome reward. If the feeling you get after winning a local league game is a total high, just imagine what it's like to beat out all the other leagues in the country to win a national championship title!

PHOTO BY FELICIA GRAHAM

THE TEXAS ROLLERGIRLS TEXECUTIONERS AND OTHER LEAGUES' TRAVEL TEAMS LOG PLENTY OF AIRLINE MILES GOING TO TOURNAMENTS AND AWAY GAMES

One of the best perks of roller derby is the rapidly growing tournament culture. Not only do you get the opportunity to travel to cities you've never seen, but you also get to meet the vast network of women who love to skate and play derby as much as you do. It is not preposterous to imagine that you might find your derby doppelganger on the starting line in San Francisco, or at the pre-game meet-n-greet in Providence. Since derby is a sport that unites like-minded individuals, tournaments and inter-league play are kind of like giant, wild family reunions, where you never know what to expect.

The first multi-league tournament was hosted from February 24 to February 26, 2006 in Tucson. Dubbed the Dust Devil, this tourney attracted the twenty charter flat track leagues of the then-new WFTDA. Fittingly, the mothers of the flat track movement, the Texas Rollergirls, were the victors of the first national title. The unsung winner at this tournament, however, was flat track derby itself. Seeing girls from locales as diverse as Madison, Seattle, Kansas City, and Atlanta meeting for the first time to toast the success of the weekend showed that the game they had been playing had just become a nationally competitive sport.

In 2007, the WFTDA held two regional qualifiers in 2007—one in Tucson, and one in Columbus, Ohio—to accommodate the growing number of member leagues. The nationals were hosted in Austin by the defending champs, the Texas Rollergirls. It was obvious that the competing leagues spent the past year wisely. The title that year was triumphantly nabbed by the underdog Kansas City Roller Warriors.

But no one league has managed to reign as a champ for too long . . . . A year later, in a shocking turn of events, Kansas City failed to even advance from their regional qualifier tournament. The leaders of the sport were shuffled again when the Gotham Girls of New York bested the Windy City Rollers of Chicago in the final game of the 2008 national tournament in Portland, Oregon. Then, in 2009, Gotham ceded the trophy to the young upstart Oly Rollers from Olympia, Washington.

The ebb and flow of dominance in the sport creates an air of the unexpected for fans, and hope for the hard working underdog teams. But, sometimes, skaters would rather scrap the serious stakes and just have a good time. For these occasions, it is not uncommon to see skaters mix it up by forming ad hoc teams with rivals from other leagues based on fun or silly themes. After a whole season of skating against the same girls, there is nothing more refreshing than being able to skate with some of your toughest competitors, instead of opposite them!

June 26, 2009, provided this opportunity at the third annual East Coast Extravaganza in Philadelphia. This tournament is a combination of WFTDA-sanctioned bouts played for national ranking, and fun expo bouts between mixed teams or non-WFTDA leagues. On the West Coast, The Big One Tournament also celebrates its third year of both sanctioned and for-fun bouts that pit many of the California leagues against one another.

Flat-trackers don't get to have all the fun, though. The weekend of June 26, 2008, played host to the first multi-league banked track tournament held by the L.A. Derby Dolls, open to both banked and flat track teams. The Lonestar Rollergirls, the San Diego Derby Dolls, and the flat-track Orange County Rollergirls picked up the gauntlet and put up a great fight. Most significantly, however, the flat track super team, Team Awesome, proved incontrovertibly that derby is derby regardless of skating surface. They came within one point of taking the trophy from L.A. The Lonestar Rollergirls continued the Battle on the Bank tradition by hosting the tournament in 2009.

Whether you are skating at a tournament for pure fun or for a shiny trophy, one fact remains the same: it's gonna be a freakin' marathon. For two to three days, you should expect to eat, drink, and breathe nothing but derby. And you'll do it playing as many as three full games in a day, up to three days in a row. For that reason, you should come prepared not just for battle, but for war. Roxy Rockett, a superheroic jammer, and all-around derby role model, from the Carolina Rollergirls shares her wisdom in a checklist for the tourney-bound skater . . .

Roxy Rockett's Advice for Tournament Travel

1. **Prepare by Watching Footage:** Watching a game in which I did especially well helps pump up my confidence, and gets me ready for the first whistle. I can watch the same bout over and over again and find new meanings behind every move. I watch the opponents' footage leading up to a tournament, but once we're done with that last practice before a tournament, I want to focus on my game more than theirs.

2. **Rest:** Sleep whenever possible. Usually I am restless, constantly thinking of situations that can arise on the track, and different ways of getting out of them. If you can't sleep, at least lie down and relax.

3. **Observe:** Watch all the other leagues' games in the tournament that you can handle without exhausting yourself. When leagues are even, skill-wise, you see a lot of new inventive strategy being done on the spot. Sometimes the skaters aren't even aware they are doing it! If you can spot those moves, and figure out how to do them, you just added ammunition to your reflex mode on the track.

4. **Equipment Check:** On the last night of practice before the tournament, double-check your skates for any possible errors that could occur. I had a stripped locknut the whole Dust Devil tournament. We didn't have the right wrench to tighten it, so after every jam I skated, I had to fix it. It was a pain in the ass! Now, I usually have a tool kit with extra kingpins, axles, nuts, bearings, and cushions that I check with my luggage.

5. **Know Your Surface:** Finding out the type of surface you'll be skating on is important to what kind of wheels you will use. I try to get info from the skater coordinator of the

hosting league. Or, I will go and look at images online of the host league during home bouts and check out the most common wheel type worn by their skaters.

6. **Uniforms:** Bringing two color versions of your uniform tops is a no-brainer, but bringing a back-up shirt the same color is also nice. It's possible some girl could grab you as she is falling, take hold of your shirt, and rip it a good bit. Or you could spill a lot of beer on it, which looks awful in photos! But, the most important thing to finalize before going into a tournament is the type of bottoms you choose. If you're trying out a new pair of shorts, underwear, or a skirt for the tourney, you want to first wear them at practice. Sprint, fall, and booty block in them just to make sure they are comfortable and non-constricting.

7. **Eat Well, Eat Often:** Focus on lots of whole grains, protein, water, and electrolytes to maintain your stamina and energy. Little snacks throughout the day always help me, too.

8. **Find Good Roommates:** When you're stacked four to a room, it's great to have some low-key roommates when you're traveling. I've had roommates that stay up all night, talking and texting on the phone, keeping me awake. I'm already nervous about the next day, so I need to have as much peace and quiet as possible. I've come to find those special skaters that I can share a room with and keep my sanity so I'll be ready to play for three days.

FAIR AND FOUL PLAY

Sanctioned violence is one of the most appealing parts of roller derby. After a crappy day of work or a fight with your girl-friend or boyfriend, it feels especially good to land a solid hit on another skater.

But we also try our best to pummel each other as safely as possible. That's why certain moves are considered legal and others will earn a skater a penalty.

Fair blocks generally break down into two basic categories—non-contact and contact (or "obstructive" and "destructive" blocking, respectively). A blocker can keep another skater from passing by getting in front of her or obstructing her path. This is also known as **positional blocking** and can be done with great effect without ever making physical contact.

Or, a skater can knock a bitch down, also known as **contact blocking**.

To make contact blocks, a skater can use her shoulders, upper arms, torso, hips, thighs, and ass. She is not allowed to use her head, lower arms, hands, feet, and definitely not her teeth. No jabbing another skater with the bony part of the elbow either. A skater can initiate a block when positioned alongside another skater or when she is positioned in front of her.

There are parts of the body that are kosher to hit and ones that aren't. For the most part, the torso, starting at the bottom of the neck and ending about halfway down the thigh, is fair game. That means hits to the tits are allowed—and yes, they hurt! According to most modern rule sets, you can't nail another skater in the head, neck, or lower part of her legs.

One of the biggest no-no's is contact blocking from behind. A skater can't ram someone in the back or knee her opponent in the ass. The basic premise here is that a skater should be able to see a hit coming so she can try and defend herself.

Back in the days of old school roller derby, skaters were known to trip each other, yank hair, and straight-arm one another in the neck (a maneuver known as "the clothesline"). These moves were choreographed in advance and such stunt hits were big crowd pleasers. But in modern day derby, we like our hits one hundred percent real and unanticipated.

That means—no choking, head butting, tripping, and absolutely no biting or eye gouging. If it looks like anything in an episode of *The Three Stooges*, it's probably not legal.

ASSISTS

Roller derby isn't just about taking skaters from the opposing team down—it's about helping the skater on your team do well, too. Moves that can be used to help your team's jammer and fellow blockers are commonly known as assists. They're fun to do and to watch.

WHIPS—One skater reaches her arm out and the other skater latches onto that arm and pulls forward. The skater with her arm out transfers her velocity to the other skater while twisting her torso. It's almost like bowling a skater along the track.

A CT ROLLERGIRLS JAMMER GRABS ASSISTANCE FROM HER BLOCKER TO SCORE AGAINST THE DOMINION DERBY GIRLS AT THE 2009 EAST COAST EXTRAVAGANZA

REVERSE WHIP—The person giving the whip skates backward and often uses both arms to whip the receiving skater forwards.

DOUBLE WHIP—Two skaters form a chain by linking arms and they whip a third skater at the end.

LEG WHIP—A skater uses her leg instead of her arm to give a whip. This move requires excellent balance!

PUSSY WHIP—Not to be confused with pussy whipped! A skater reaches her arm through her teammate's legs, latches on to her crotch and gives a good solid tug, using that momentum to pick up speed. Perhaps not the most effective assist move, but a titillating one to say the least.

WAITRESS WHIP—One skater whips another skater forward and when that skater moves beyond her partner, she turns around and offers both arms to pull the first skater forward.

BUMPS—When a skater uses one or two hands to push another skater forward and increase her speed.

TEXAS ROLLERGIRLS' DINAH-MITE BLOCKS WINDY CITY'S VARLA VENDETTA OUT OF BOUNDS

PHOTO BY JULES DOYLE

OUT OF BOUNDS

For play to be considered legal, a skater must be within certain boundaries. In flat track derby it's quite common for a skater to be blocked so hard that she goes careening off the track and into the lap of an adoring audience member.

Skaters can also get knocked out of bounds in banked track derby. A well-timed block can send a skater flying up and over the rails. She'll catch some air and, if she's lucky, land on her feet once she hits the ground. It's quite a dramatic sight when a skater flies off the track.

In both versions of roller derby, when a skater is blocked to the infield, she can't just get back on the track anywhere she likes. She must re-enter the pack without advancing her position—there's no cutting along the inside of the track. Advancing position when re-entering the track will result in penalties (and usually vocal obscenities from the opposing team)!

Even when they're in the boundary lines, blockers and pivots need to stay within twenty feet of the pack in order to legally block or assist another skater. Breaking this rule will also result in a penalty (and again, more ire from opponents).

PASSING THE STAR

Usually only a jammer can score points for her team. But there is one unique situation in which a pivot can become the point scorer. As you'll recall, there are only two positions that wear the helmet panties: the pivots with the stripe down the middle and the jammers with the stars on the side. There is a special play called "Passing the Star" that allows the jammer to remove her helmet panty and hand it over to the pivot. When this happens, the pivot then becomes the jammer and is able to score for her team.

This move isn't used often and for good reason. If the panty is dropped or knocked to the ground while being passed to the pivot, that team will likely have to skate an entire lap around before

RAT CITY ROLLERGIRLS' CARMEN GETDONE PERFORMS THE RARE BUT EFFECTIVE PASSING OF THE STAR TO TEAMMATE FEMME FATALE

PHOTO BY JOE SCHWARTZ

they can try making the hand-off again. But if done smoothly, passing the star is a great way to confuse the other team. After all, they've been focusing on blocking one jammer and suddenly they have to re-adjust for a new target!

BUT WAIT . . . THERE'S MORE!

Are there more rules? Hell yes, and plenty of them. There are regulations for when you can put your helmet panty on during a jam; for what happens when a ref mistakenly blows the whistle; for what to do when a skater is bleeding . . . There are even rules about how large the numbers on the back of a skater's uniform have to be.

Derby girls definitely have to engage their minds as well as their bodies if they want to truly understand the game and skate penalty-free. If you want to go deeply into the minutiae of roller derby rules, you can check out WFTDA's online rules forum (http://rules.wftda.com/) or get in touch with your local league, who will probably be happy to give you a copy of their rule set.

STRATEGY

Over the years, like any athletes, skaters have spent countless hours cooking up strategies to try and crush their rivals. They've pored over white boards and drilled plays over and over to the point where they could probably skate them in their sleep.

Strategies can help a team learn how to work together and they can catch an opposing team off guard. We could fill an entire book with strategies we've tried over the years—some that worked magnificently and others that were catastrophes on wheels.

But if we told you all our secrets, we'd have to kill you. So, here we'll just give you a taste—a little strategy known as "Runaway Pussy." Let's say the Hellcats and the Holy Rollers of the TXRD Lonestar Rollergirls are playing against each other. And during one jam, the jammer from the Holy Rollers is approaching the pack for the second time far ahead of the Hellcats' jammer. The Hellcats' jammer has just taken a nasty fall and is having trouble picking up speed again. It may be time to cut losses and just make sure the Holy Rollers don't score.

In this instance, the Hellcats blockers might decide to skate as fast as they can, making it difficult for the Holy Rollers' jammer to catch up, let alone pass them. This move is called Runaway Pussy because you are basically running away from the competition. And frankly, it's a pussy maneuver because real blockers stick around for the fight. Some leagues have gone so far as to create rules banning this play.

When we train skaters, we advise them to approach each jam with some sort of strategy. Blockers should come up with a game plan for who will work defensively and who will work offensively and which position within the pack each will play.

That said, anything could happen in a jam. Experienced skaters will know when to stick to the game plan and when to ditch it and make one up on the fly. And a great team will know how to communicate with each other during a jam. They'll talk to one another, yell commands, grab each other (which is legal, if you are on the same team), and come up with a game plan to respond to whatever the present circumstances are.

PENALTIES

You break the rules, you pay the price. And in derby that price is a penalty. There are two types of penalties, minor and major. Different leagues handle penalties in different ways, but there's a fair chance that if a skater earns one, she'll have to sit out for a while (usually a minute) in the penalty box, a.k.a. the sin bin.

Of course, for each second she's gone, her team has one less skater in play. And, if the jammer from the other team laps the entire pack, she'll automatically pick up points for the ones in the sin bin (these are known as ghost points). If a skater racks up a substantial number of penalties, she may be ejected from the game. In that case she is forced to leave the track for the remainder of the bout.

Most penalties are earned through illegal blocks. Nail someone with an elbow or your noggin, you'll earn a penalty. Same goes for cutting the track or beating a skater when she's already down. Penalties will be doled out for misconduct, too. Yes, this is slightly ironic in a sport where skaters are actually named Miss Conduct, Auntie Establishment, and Bea Naughty. But even in roller derby, we maintain a bit of decorum. Flipping off the opposing team too many times will land a skater in trouble. And if a skater doesn't like the ref's call and decides to respond with a choice piece of vocabulary, she can expect even more time in the penalty box.

For most leagues, the penalty box is a chair or bench where skaters must serve their time. But remember that when modern roller derby first began in Austin, they came up with a more creative form of punishment—the penalty wheel.

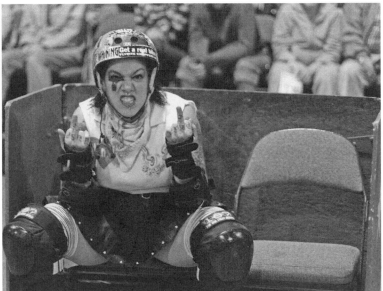

HISPANIC PANIC OF TXRD LONESTAR ROLLERGIRLS IN THE PENALTY BOX

PENALTY WHEEL

As you may recall the penalty wheel is like a sadistic version of the Wheel of Fortune, with the names of various punishments painted on it. A penalty mistress, often dressed in dominatrix attire, spins the wheel. The offending skater then has to obey whatever command the wheel lands on, including tasks like jousting (on skates), pillow fighting, and arm wrestling.

At the beginning of modern day roller derby, the penalty wheel was a fun way for gals to get a quick break from skating and entertain the audience. But many skaters now see penalty wheels as detracting from the true athleticism of the sport.

FIGHTING

Much like in hockey and wrestling, the early days of roller derby were famous for knock down, drag out fights. The crowds roared with approval when skaters got so riled up, they completely forgot about the jam and started pounding and tackling each other to the ground instead.

In today's derby, there is great and ongoing debate about fighting.

Those who support the idea will often tell you that crowds *love* fights. And that's a hard one to argue with since many warm-blooded Americans find catfights hot.

As for the skaters, we take this sport very seriously and when someone breaks the rules or we're just fed up with another skater's attitude, the temptation to tussle can easily arise.

Fighting during bouts, we should mention, usually means wrestling and a few bonks on the helmet (which actually don't hurt at all). We don't punch each other in the face or knee each other in the groin.

Well, most of us don't.

Many skaters who go in for the occasional brawl will tell you it's a great stress reliever. Some say scrapping during a bout prevents much more serious and real fights after the game is done.

Others argue that fighting takes away from the genuine athletic skill involved in roller derby. They prefer getting their aggression out by beating their competitors, not by beating up their competitors. Still other skaters find fighting objectionable for feminist reasons—it's a little too close to activities like oil or mud wrestling for comfort and they would prefer avoiding a scenario that potentially objectifies women.

In modern day derby, the non-fighting camp currently prevails. According to both WFTDA and most banked track rules, fighting will automatically get you ejected from a game. But fighting still happens in some forms of derby, most notably in Renegade Roller Derby.

RENEGADE ROLLER DERBY

Back in the summer of 2004, a number of skaters who had been skating with Arizona Roller Derby in Phoenix, mostly members of AZRD's French Kiss Army team, decided to break off from their league. The split was largely due to philosophical differences about the future of the sport. The skaters who left formed a league of their own and called themselves the Renegade Rollergirls.

Their emblem is a hand grenade, and as it and their name imply, Renegade Derby is quite explosive. There are no penalties in Renegade Derby, so the game moves fast and just about anything goes. Skaters can trip each other, side-tackle, and jab with their elbows. One Renegade named Mayhemily is known to play without wearing a helmet.

For the most part, the Renegades play on a flat track, but they have a longstanding challenge to bout on "any surface, any time." Fights are fairly common, too, though the referees tend to break them up quickly. Renegade may sound like an especially dangerous form of the sport. But, says JoAnn Thraxx, one of the Renegades' founding members, injuries are no more common in this no holds barred version of the sport than they are in mainstream roller derby.

PHOTO BY NICK LOVELL

RENEGADE ROLLERGIRLS

Their attitude is akin to the Golden Rule. As Thraxx explains, "You don't do something you wouldn't want someone to do to you. For example, I wouldn't punch someone else in the face because I still have to look pretty when I go into work on Monday."

This outlaw version of derby has caught on in other states. There are now a number of Renegade leagues in Oregon, Southern California, and Virginia.

Derby Crushes, Wives, and Weddings

THOUGH ROLLERGIRLS SMACK EACH other around on the track and often manage to get into some pretty heated debates off the track, it's safe to say there's a lot more love in this sport than hate. That love can manifest itself in many ways. Here are a few we find worth noting.

Derby Crush

A derby crush is much like a regular crush. It's that indescribable tingly feeling you get when you see that someone special. In derby, the only difference is that in addition to thinking your crush is totally adorable and has a super swell personality, your emotions may also be influenced by the person's ability to skate.

Derby Wife

Chances are you'll make plenty of friends in roller derby. But if you're really lucky, you'll find a derby wife. This term was first coined by Kasey Bomber during that historic 2003 trip to Arizona. The words "derby wife" were the best way she could express how she felt about fellow L.A. Derby Doll Evil E.

As Evil E puts it, a derby wife is like a Laverne to your Shirley, a Siegfried to your Roy, a Jack to your Coke. Still not sure you understand the concept? Here are a few guidelines:

1. She is the one person in this whole sport of roller derby that the very instant you looked at her, you felt like you'd known her since you were a newborn. She looked just like your best friend from fifth grade, or something she did reminded you of all the things you ever liked in anyone else.

2. She is the first person you'd call if you ever need to get bailed out of jail.
3. She's the one who will be holding back your hair when you puke after drinking too much, and she won't let anyone take your picture while doing it.
4. She'll ride in the ambulance with you when you lose a tooth, break your wrist, or tear your ACL. She'll make you laugh the whole way to the hospital, try to steal your pain medication (lovingly), and sneak your favorite food and a beer into recovery.
5. She'll make her actual spouse understand that if (s)he loves her, (s)he's gonna have to put up with you, too, no matter how many times you come over forcing her or him to revisit all the derby-related shows on the TiVo that you missed.
6. She may not even be your best friend in the league or the sport, but she'd be the one you know will be the first one to back you up, even if you're dead wrong. She'll just tell you you've lost your fucking mind later in private, possibly kick your ass a little bit, and then be the only one who could ever talk your hotheaded ass into some reason.

Some gals take multiple wives, often from different leagues. (In a sport filled with so many great women, you didn't honestly expect us to be monogamous, did you?) In addition to her fabulous derby wife, Kitty Scratch, Axles also has a derby mistress—her Lone Star soul mate, Karma. Derby teams have decided to enter holy matrimony with other teams. An entire league (Emerald City Rollergirls) has taken on Goody Two Skates of Rose City Rollers as their collective wife.

How do you make such relations official? As with any good nuptials, in Vegas, of course! Back in 2005, as preparations were being made for the first ever RollerCon,

PHOTO BY BOSS HOG

Axles had an idea—why not have a Derby Wedding? That summer, more than eighty couples (and a few threesomes) gathered in front of skater Deez Nutz, dressed in her Elvis impersonator best. Some were dressed in Salvation Army bridal rejects, several were wearing skates, and one crafty derby bride made a train out of toilet paper. They all recited these vows:

Dearly Beloved, Ladies and Broads . . .

We're gathered here tonight to honor the union of these skaters in the grand tradition of derby marriage.

As you look to your future wife or wives next to you, know that you are entering a very unique and special union.

It is one based not only on friendship, honor, and loyalty, but also on tricking each other into ill-advised late night situations, reminding each other to always recall with relish your best take-down if ever you doubt your skill before a bout, and advising you to always select the "daily digest" option on all twenty-nine of your Yahoo groups.

The skater or skaters beside you may not be your best friends, but they have that special quality that no other in roller derby possesses for you. They are the ones who "complete you." They are also the ones who will not hesitate to punch you in the mouth if you ever said that out loud. So, without further ado, please join hands and repeat after me:

I, [state your name] take you, [state your partner's name], to be my derby wife.

I promise to ride with you in the ambulance if you ever break your arm in a bout even if the EMTs are all ugly.

I will always tell you when your pads start to smell like a goat's ass in summer.

I vow to always take pictures up your skirt at after-parties, and to hold your hair back while you puke on the sidewalk.

I will always be your first phone call from jail, even if I was the one who got you there in the first place.

I will always remind you about the amazing last bout if non-skating matters start to annoy you.

I promise to be your biggest fan . . . unless we face off in a bout. Then I promise to hit you harder than anyone else on your team, because I'd never insult you by going easy.

So, with the power vested in me by Ivanna S. Pankin, the Double Down Saloon, and Col. Tom Parker, I now pronounce you derby wives.

You may kiss the brides.

AM I a DERby GiRL?

CAROLINA ROLLERGIRLS'
LADY SMACKBETH AT
YOUR SERVICE

ASK ME? ABOUT ★ ROLLER DERBY

PHOTO BY PRACHI GUARIAR

IF READING THE rules of the game didn't scare you away, you might now be asking yourself, "Am *I* a derby girl?"

We remember very vividly the days we asked ourselves that same question. We both wondered if we would be tough enough, athletic enough, rock-n-roll enough, or hot enough to stand up to the other derby girls.

Back then, in 2003, the L.A. Derby Dolls league was only months old, still skating with its figurative training wheels. We had no notion of what to expect when we showed up to our first practices. One of us was a lapsed athlete worried that she'd encounter a rogue pack of SuicideGirls in an inked up beauty

DOWN AND DERBY

108

contest on wheels. The other was a 5′2″ thirty-one-year-old, fairly certain that her size and childhood dread of P.E. class would make her instant meat in an Amazon sandwich.

We arrived at Skateland, the Derby Dolls' practice venue back then, where an unlikely shift change was about to occur. Deep in the heart of the San Fernando Valley, the parking lot was teeming with excited women waiting to begin practice, looking as though all they had in common were their ovaries and the skates slung over their shoulders. Strains of Christian rap music filtered out of the front doors, accompanying an exodus of teenaged holy rollers and making way for the entering derby hopefuls.

We met brainiacs, brickhouses, and will-o'-the-wisps. We laced up next to tattooed punk rockers and elementary school teachers, cops and reformed delinquents, loudmouths and wallflowers. We were relieved to realize even though there were tough girls who embodied all our imagined fears, there were also plenty of others who looked just like us. They also skated just like us—which at that point, wasn't saying all that much.

Then again, back in our early days of skating, things weren't quite what they are today. This version of roller derby was so new and skaters were so scarce that if you showed up— Congratulations! You were on a team. In more recent years, the standard of play has escalated to heights of athleticism scarcely imagined back when we first ironed out our strides. To watch a game today—with all the screaming fans, jarring collisions, and lightning strategy—and think, "Hey, I can do this starting tomorrow!" is truly a brave aspiration.

The skaters in their war paint and personalized uniforms look like a gang straight out of *The Warriors*. They are intimidating. The action is raw, and painful-looking. Bones are broken on a regular basis. This is something that people do for fun? You're damn right it is. Catch a skater coming off the track after a game and look in her eyes, and you'll see something confident and attractive. That's called pride. Tenacious new girls by the dozens step up every month to learn how to get that look for themselves.

Of course, it had to be more than quads and chromosomes that brought us all to the rink, right? Is it an elusive set of inner desires, something wrong in our heads, or perhaps a genetic disposition to be a capital-B Badass? Maybe it's an outlet for people who like to think of the word "can't" as a challenge rather than as a dead end. Or an all-consuming hobby for those who have always wanted more than they were allowed, and weren't afraid to get physical to get it.

Natily Blair, a.k.a. Ginger Snap, of the Gotham Girls Roller Derby, once put it, "You don't become a rollergirl, really, you realize that you are one already." But maybe you're still not sure if this describes you. Maybe you are still asking yourself if you have it in you. If you haven't already run out to buy your first eight wheels, maybe this quiz we've devised can help you decide.

1. What is the first thing that comes to mind when you think of roller skates?
   a) Jam skating to Michael Jackson's "Thriller" at the local rink when you were a kid.
   b) That *Baywatch*-esque rollerblading phase you were in back in the early nineties.

c) The horrific memory of all those skating parties you spent clinging to the wall as a child.

2. Which of these best describes the amount of free time in your schedule?
   a) Let's put it this way, I've seen way too many reruns of *The Golden Girls* lately, so I'm wide open for an exciting hobby.
   b) I'm pretty busy with work and family, but I still try to take some time for myself.
   c) Things are crazy; I barely have time to answer this survey.

3. What would you do if you got a black eye?
   a) Immediately take a picture of it and put it up as your Facebook default.
   b) Slap a steak on it and hope it goes away before anyone starts to worry about you.
   c) Stay home until you could cover it with makeup, because you can't stand going out looking less than perfect.

4. How would you describe yourself socially?
   a) I'm the life of every party. I love to be the center of attention . . . or so I'm told when I wake up in the yard wearing someone else's pants.
   b) I can seem a little shy when you meet me, but I come out of my shell after a while. Or after a few tequila shots.
   c) I try to avoid crowds, because strangers really creep me out.

5. Your friends invite you on an extreme sports vacation: how do you react?
   a) Heck yeah, man! I'll try anything once, and probably twice. Let's go, like, yesterday.
   b) I'm not into sports, but my friends are fun, so I'll give it a shot.

c) I don't like sweating, and team sports are totally gay, forget it.

6. When you see an Ultimate Fighting Championship match on television, what do you do?
a) Play a drinking game for each time someone bleeds.
b) Pretend to be reading your copy of *US Weekly*, but take note of a few good moves for self-defense.
c) Iron your tie-dyed "Give Peace a Chance" t-shirt, then go out and combat senseless violence with free hugs.

If you answered "a" to most of these questions, you are definitely roller derby material. You are no stranger to roller skates, you're not afraid to get out there and try new and potentially dangerous things, and you've got time to devote to a new hobby. Essentially, you have "Potential Derby Cult Recruit" tattooed all over you.

If you answered "b" to most of these questions, there's hope for you for sure! You might not think you are very bold and adventurous, but that fire in you isn't just heartburn. Trade those roller blades in for quads and introduce yourself to your inner badass.

If you answered "c" to most of these questions, roller derby might not be for you. It looks like your schedule may not permit you the practice you need, and the potential for injury in front of a big crowd could scare you off derby. But, if the fact that we just suggested that you *can't* do this makes you so irritated that you want to try anyway . . . there might just be a rollergirl in you yet!

PROFILE: Queen Elizabitch

PHOTO BY MARTY WESTRA

Sioux Falls, South Dakota, population 154,997, is a lovely place to live. It has been named by *Forbes* as the "#1 Best Small Place for Business and Careers" for five years running. In the 2006 "United States Drinking Water Quality Study Report," Sioux Falls was also ranked third in the country for cleanest drinking water.

Well, sure. Clean water and small business is great and all, but Elizabeth Nelson thought that roller derby would be a much more exciting way to put her small Midwest town on the map. Nelson, a.k.a. Queen Elizabitch, a former competitive figure skater, helped create the Sioux Falls Roller Dollz.

Q: Why did you want to start a roller derby league in Sioux Falls?

QUEEN ELIZABITCH: I wanted to start roller derby because I didn't have any friends in South Dakota. I moved back here from Phoenix and fell in love with derby when I watched AZRD. Now that it's all started and rollin' (pardon the pun), I continue to do it because it keeps me in shape, is a healthy channel for my aggression, and, really, it's an excuse to wear fishnets and mini shorts on the daily!

Q: What is the closest league to yours?

QE: Sioux City Roller Dames are over an hour away. But before they were in existence it was Omaha, which is two and a half hours.

Q: *Did you get any help from skaters with any of the more established leagues as you were starting up?*

QE: The Minnesota Roller Girls helped us immensely in our development stage. Especially Jawbreaker (now with the North Star Rollergirls) . . . she's been an incredible mentor for our league and is willing to do whatever it takes to help us when we need her. She Who Cannot Be Named, from Rocky Mountain Roller Girls, has been great at guiding us through our application to WFTDA and has always been quick to answer frantic questions.

Q: *What are some of the challenges of running a derby league in a smaller town?*

QE: We have a small pool of potential skaters to pick from. We run a league with about twenty full-time, healthy skaters . . . fourteen of those are on the "travel" team. Another challenge is education . . . we're constantly trying to educate the community of the fact that we're not out to just wail on each other. All of us want to be taken seriously as athletes, but the local media is more interested in the fluffiness of roller derby (giving back to the community and being a women's group) and not so much in the fact that we're legit and want to be in the freaking sports page! There are also a lot of other sports teams in our city that make it difficult to pull fans away from. Our fan base overlaps with that of the indoor football league (though they pull in five thousand fans a game), and we really wish we could have a partnership instead of a competition with them.

Q: *What are some of the advantages?*

QE: We do have a few advantages . . . such as the fact that we're the only game in town—if you want to see roller derby, you have to come to us! Also, Sioux Falls is a pretty supportive little community. If you've got a good idea and have a plan in place, the citizens will support you. We have had great support from local community leaders and

feel like as long as we keep giving back,
the city will continue to stand behind us.

We also have a great relationship with local
morning radio shows that allows us to come on air
every Friday morning to promote whatever we want. In
a larger city, this would not be the case. We don't pay a
dime and receive oodles and oodles of free promotion!

Q: What kind of venue do you skate in?

QE: We skate in a venue titled Expo Ice which is an ice arena/horse
barn/roller skating rink! In the winter they keep ice down for hockey
games and in the summer they put dirt in to hold horse shows. When
we want to hold bouts, we take the ice/dirt out and lay down our track.
We lovingly refer to this venue as our barn. All of our bouts smell like
horse shit. No joke, it's hilarious.

Q: What's your average attendance?

QE: Twelve hundred and fifty.

**Q: Do you think that skating derby in a smaller town is different from
skating in a bigger one?**

QE: It's so different! We are so much more visible here! I mean, if one
of us fucks up, we are all in trouble. For instance, one girl gets arrested
for something non–derby related. Say she's not even wearing derby
gear . . . the media finds out the name of this individual and that
she's a member of the Roller Dollz, next thing you know newspaper
headlines read "Roller Doll Gets Arrested" and then we spend ninety
percent of our time doing recon work . . . *that* is annoying.

Still with us? If so, you are ready for step two. You should know that, like the Bible, derby also has ten commandments. They represent the elements that will always be true about the sport no matter where you play, or whom you skate with, and that must be accepted before you can become a happy and effective wheeled warrior.

FIRST COMMANDMENT:
THERE IS NO PART-TIME IN ROLLER DERBY.

This is rule number one, because if you think that you are picking up a fun little hobby, you don't know the half of it.

The simple truth of the matter is that roller derby is time consuming. A typical roller derby week might include two practices, a game, and at least one committee meeting. Most current roller derby leagues require a minimum of six to ten practices a month, not counting special team practices and meetings, or game days.

In addition, in order to run a D.I.Y. league, the skaters must also moonlight as business owners to keep that league afloat. You can rest assured that any professional skill you have will find a home in at least one roller derby committee. Committees can tackle everything from sponsorship to merchandising, uniforms to training coordination, and event planning to accounting.

Also, nothing caps off a good meeting, practice, or game like a nightcap, or a late night snack at the local hangout. After spending all this time with such committed and multi-talented women, you probably won't want to miss out on any of the social stuff either. This, of course, is pretty much considered more derby time —just ask your loved ones.

And don't expect to become a part of the group without pulling your weight. If you take the commitment, make the commitment. Don't expect to be able to cash in on all the fun stuff without getting your hands dirty doing some manual labor. We can smell a derby dilettante a mile away. They don't smell good.

SECOND COMMANDMENT:
ROLLER DERBY IS A SPORT.

Although the bumps and jumps of roller derby might be wrapped in a fashionable package and filled with playful names and characters, rest assured that underneath all that flash is a lot of hard work. Re-learning to live your life on eight wheels can be as daunting as learning another language. It's not all enamored fans and media opportunities. Those in it strictly for the perks are always sniffed out and given the bum's rush before long.

Even learning the game itself can be tricky. Remember all that stuff from the last chapter? You will not only be responsible for knowing and understanding each of your league's rules, but will be expected to put them into practice every time your wheels touch the track. Think of it like studying for your favorite class. Only this time, instead of learning state capitals or the square root of 7,225, your test will come in not letting your ass meet the ground the first time you're hit.

Get ready to see some changes in the mirror, too. If you take a moment to imagine the athletes in other sports, you will see that each athlete is tailored to the sport they play through training. Most basketball players are lean and fluid. Swimmers are broad in the shoulders and narrow across the hips. Roller derby, like other sports, will have its own effect on your body. As you train tirelessly you might find that the constant requirement to turn left on the track leaves one leg slightly stronger than the other. Axles had to return a perfect pair of pink leather go-go boots her husband gave her once she realized they fit her right calf beautifully, but couldn't be zipped over her pumped up left one!

You might also notice that your butt cheeks have raised an inch or two in the seat of your pants. And you might feel one day that your ankles are strong enough to support the Brooklyn Bridge at rush hour.

SUZY HOTROD OF GOTHAM
GIRLS ROLLER DERBY

THIRD COMMANDMENT:
YOU WILL GET FRUSTRATED.

Even those who have backgrounds in rink skating and artistic roller skating soon learn that translating skating skills into this team sport can be a wildly different animal. Before your face makes it to a trading card, you've got a hard road of practices to learn the skills of the game.

Inevitably, there will be one or two skills that will completely elude you for months or even years, no matter how many times you attempt them. But no matter how frustrated you get, you have to dig out the determination to keep trying until you get it right.

It's a lot like learning to play guitar. Just when you think you've got all those open chords down, you move on to the awkward crazy-making barre chords. For months they sound like the washboard in a jug band, and you think you'll never get them to ring. But one day, out of nowhere, they suddenly start to sing as easy as Lionel Richie on a Sunday morning.

With practice, practice, and more practice, your derby skills will arrive. Luckily, at least until then, you get to kill some frustration by wailing on your teammates!

FOURTH COMMANDMENT:
YOU WILL FALL DOWN.

If there is one constant in this sport, it is falling. After all, the whole goal of the blocker is to effectively stop the opposing team from advancing on the track. What could be more effective than knocking someone on their ass? With as many as four bloodthirsty skaters gunning for you at any time, you can expect to get used to hitting the ground hard. Bruises are par for the course, and the terms "track rash" and "wheel bang" will become frequent visitors to your conversation. Because of this, roller derby is *not* for the weak-hearted.

DIESEL OF THE ANGEL CITY DERBY GIRLS TAKES A TUMBLE

FIFTH COMMANDMENT:
YOU WILL GET HURT.

Broken ankles, torn tendons, snapped collarbones, and dislocated shoulders are just some of the injuries that top the list of rollergirl maladies. Although you will be taught safe methods of falling to avoid serious injury, you must always know that injury is a possibility and a probability. For this reason, personal health insurance is always a good thing to have at the top of your rollergirl checklist. Most leagues will also require that you get insurance offered by the USA Roller Sports (USARS) organization for a nominal yearly fee.

Another question you must seriously consider is whether you'll be okay at your job if you have to endure, say, six weeks in a cast. Do you have a job that requires the use of both hands, such as hairdresser, animator, or bus driver? Do you need both legs to make a living? Are you a construction worker, a retail sales-person, or a tour guide? Moreover, do you have children who would be traumatized if mommy came home with a black eye or stitches? Several skaters we know have not only had wounds to nurse during a game, but also a scared and upset child to heal afterward as well.

Countless rollergirls take these sorts of gambles at practice every day. Their passion for the sport gives them no choice but to train for safety and hope for the best. But it is a worry they live with constantly.

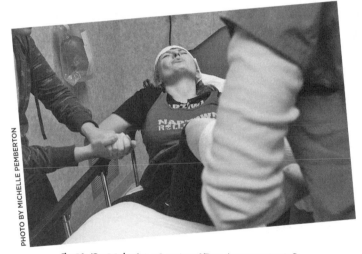

STRAWBERRY JAM OF THE NAPTOWN ROLLERGIRLS IN THE HOSPITAL WITH A BROKEN ANKLE

AM I A DERBY GIRL?

121

PROFILE: Tequila Mockingbird

PHOTO BY DAKOTA "KOLA LOKA" PROSCH

Attorney Tahirah Johnson, a.k.a. Tequila Mockingbird, is one of those rollergirls who were already very active and athletic by the time she found derby. She was an avid cyclist, weight-lifter, boxer, and even an occasional break-dancer before landing a spot on the Windy City Rollers' team The Fury.

What happened to Tequila on August 25, 2007, is an anomaly in the world of derby. But it's also a very real reminder that the sport we play is a dangerous one.

Q: How did you get involved in derby?

TEQUILA MOCKINGBIRD: In 2004, I was living in Chicago and the Windy City Rollers were just getting started. I saw a recruiting flyer at a club and they were having a get-together the following week. I went to a workout they had in Wicker Park and stayed with them for the next three years.

DOWN AND DERBY

Q: *What about derby appealed to you?*

TM: It sounded tough and fun. I had run a few marathons, but that was rough on my knees. And I'd never done any team sports before.

Q: *What positions did you play?*

TM: I did a lot of pivoting, but played all three positions. Pivoting was just the role I had the most fun doing. Being the brains of the pack was what came most naturally of the three roles.

Q: *Were you ever concerned about the dangers of playing a full contact sport?*

TM: I didn't worry too much about it because it's usually not too violent and you wear so much protective gear. Usually the worst-case scenarios were a broken leg or ankle; one woman had a broken nose. There's always danger in sports—even in long distance running people have died. I don't normally dwell on such things.

Q: *In the summer of 2007, your team, The Fury, played a bout against The Double Crossers. At the beginning of the second half of the game, you got hurt. What happened?*

TM: I was falling backward and a lot of people around me were falling, too. I got hit in the back of the neck with a toe-stop, and it snapped my neck and rolled into my spinal cord.

Luckily, skater Varla Vendetta's parents go to every game. Her dad is a doctor and her mom is a nurse, so they told the paramedics where to take me. Her mom knew which hospital nearby was the best.

Q: *What was going through your mind at the time?*

TM: I couldn't wiggle my toes or fingers or anything. I was in shock. When they were wheeling me down the hospital hall I remember asking the doctors "You're

123

not going to cut my hair are you?" I still had my vanity intact. You want to go into your grave as a cool derby chick.

Q: The injury damaged one of your cervical vertebrae and initially you lost the use of both legs and could only move your left arm. How is your recovery coming along?

TM: Through physical therapy, I'm able to walk a little bit with a walker. I practice standing. I do a lot of sit-ups every day and a lot of leg workouts. It's progressing well, but I can't do much of anything on my own.

Q: What are your goals for the future?

TM: Eventually to be independent would be nice. I'd like to get into disability law so I could help people injured at a high level of disability, like myself. People with brain injuries, stroke or spinal cord damage, they really need advocates. It's difficult not to have an advocate right by your side.

Q: When you got hurt, you didn't have primary insurance. Between the medical bills and not being able to work, the costs have added up quite a bit. But the derby community has been raising money for you?

TM: Yes, they held quite a few fundraisers in Chicago that were a huge help. The Windy City Rollers referee Doris Day of the Dead and her mom made a beautiful quilt with derby-inspired fabric that they auctioned off and the winning bidder was nice enough to give it back to the league. They've held raffles at RollerCon and people have passed the hat at local bouts.

Windy City Roller Kola Loka set up a Facebook application where users can donate two dollars for the two-year anniversary of my injury. So far, the derby community has raised more than $12,000 on my behalf.

Q: *What advice would you give to other derby girls about the risk involved in this sport?*

TM: I personally don't worry too much about stuff like that. I wouldn't discourage anyone.

If you'd like to learn how to help support Tahirah's recovery, visit www.helptequila.com.

Tequila's injury is certainly one of the most extreme examples of what can happen in roller derby, but a very real reminder that we play a violent contact sport.

Doctor Stuart Willick at the University of Utah has conducted a major survey of the injury rates in roller derby. He found that nearly eighty percent of the injuries that happen are acute traumatic ones. The most common injuries are ones to the knee, ankle, shoulder, and tailbone. Seventy percent of those who reported injury said they hadn't fully recovered from the hurt they sustained.

Hopefully, improvements in training and the work of folks like Dr. Willick can reduce the rate of injury in derby. But there's no doubt the sport will always remain a dangerous one.

SIXTH COMMANDMENT:
THERE'S NO "SORRY" IN ROLLER DERBY.

If someone fell in a game, chances are some chick just knocked her down. Blockers hit. That's their job. They exist to be the immovable object that bitch-slaps the movable forces of her opponents with hips, body checks, and solid shoulders.

There are not many times in life when you can say that you've performed your job with excellence after you've hit someone so hard that they flew over a rail. But, such hits are one of the best parts of the game and are to be celebrated! If you were a lawyer who won a case, would you apologize to opposing counsel? Furthermore would opposing counsel want the pity nod? We think not on both counts. Just the same, skaters don't apologize for good clean hits.

Many times, even legal hits will lead to someone getting injured. While it is definitely a dark moment to realize that

PHOTO BY CRAIG LAMMES

you've caused the pain and suffering of your friend and fellow skater, just remember that this is a known risk. Of course, an offer to help alleviate that pain with ice, a shot of Jack Daniels, or a ride to the emergency room is always appreciated, but clean skating is blameless. It happens, and you shouldn't beat yourself up for it.

Skaters known for their hard hits on the track are supportive and generous off the track, as seen in this moment between Charm City Roller Girls' Bambi's Revenge and Just Carol.

SEVENTH COMMANDMENT: ROLLER DERBY IS A *TEAM* SPORT.

You know the old saying, "there is no 'I' in team?" Well, there is no "I" in derby, either. Current derby leagues in the U.S. and abroad can easily boast memberships of around a hundred skaters per league. No matter how much you may think you are the next shining star of the sport, you are not doing it alone.

Just like a quarterback couldn't win a football game without a receiver to run his passes to the end zone, a jammer can't exist without her blockers, and blockers can't work alone. Also, the game can't come to be without the work of referees and tireless behind-the-scenes production crews. Because of this, derby is a team sport on every level, and dependent on your ability to work well with others.

Because most leagues are self-operating affairs, patience, cooperation, and occasional humility are also required to maintain a functional league. The template for successful leagues is constantly evolving, so debates over protocol often get either tedious or heated. Since roller derby attracts a bevy of strong personalities, expect each of the above three gentle qualities to be exercised as much as your thighs. Neither hot-dogging on the track nor an "I'm-always-right" attitude in the boardroom will get you far.

EIGHTH COMMANDMENT:
THIS AIN'T FIGHT CLUB. YOU *DO* TALK ABOUT DERBY . . .
ALL. THE. TIME.

Remember all those interesting subjects you used to explore during dinner party conversations and quiet pillow talk with your sweetie? Wave good-bye.

Joining derby is like meeting someone new and falling in love. All you can talk and think about is that person. You suddenly want to rename your kitten Mr. Loverpants III and start writing earnest poetry. Meanwhile, your friends are all about one more audible sigh away from wringing your neck.

There is a certain catatonic thousand-yard stare that boyfriends, girlfriends, and derby spouses across the country have developed when their darlings start talking shop. It's a look that indicates the realization that their awesome relationship just became a threesome with roller derby. And they're not sure which one of the trio wears the pants. Many a relationship has been strained to the limit by the constant competition for attention. However, others have flourished when supportive loved ones joined what they couldn't beat by taking valuable roles of their own within the leagues.

But, don't feel too guilty about your enthusiasm! Countless strangers sitting next to you on the subway, your local dive bar, or your gynecologist's waiting room will return it to you. Wear team flair out in public or sport a derby-themed tattoo and it has the effect of sending an Evite to an inquisition. Questions ranging from the uber-enthusiastic ("OMG! What team are you on?"); to the curious ("There's roller derby in this city? Where?"); to the misguided ("But what do you do with the ball?"); to the inane ("Aren't all roller derby girls lesbians?") will play and replay until you wish you had a pocket FAQ sheet to provide to everyone in the room.

What do you care? You are in love, and you could talk track for hours on end. Fortunately, you've just gained thousands of new sisters who are dying to listen.

Derby Widows

YOU KNOW THAT LINE, "Behind every great man there stands a great woman?" Well, in derby, behind many skaters there is a great guy or gal at home. And usually this person is simultaneously thrilled that their loved one has found a hobby as cool as roller derby and bummed out that this new hobby means they hardly see their sweetie anymore.

Paramours of derby girls are often called derby widows or derby widowers. The life of a derby widow can be rough. Thankfully, Helen Fury of the Birmingham Blitz Derby Dames in England wrote a little survival guide for her widow, Ruth. Fury was kind enough to share it with us.

A Roller Derby Widow's GUIDE TO THE GRIEF PROCESS

So, fellas, and some lucky ladies, your partner has joined the derby. You thought it would be fun for your woman to pick up a new sport, and now you sit in a house full of sexy hosiery wondering when you will see your partner again. This is a challenging time fraught with confusion and loneliness. Know that you are not alone. The mourning process is real. Every widow's experience is unique, but you may recognize the following:

Denial: Many of us are ashamed to admit that early in the derby widow experience, it is actually exciting. Suddenly, it's okay to watch a mass of women in short skirts plow into each other without turning off the Internet browser filter. Your home is often filled with your wife's hot, hilarious teammates. Your lover's fitness is advancing at an astonishing rate, she's taken over changing tires, and she seems to have found an inexplicable comfort with firearms. When she drags you to the local all-night roller disco, you beam with pride at her skating skills.

Anger: It's 9:30 PM and you haven't seen Mademoiselle de Derby since yesterday. The house is littered with skates or wrist guards that smell like week-old road kill that previously subsisted on a diet of Limburger. She's spending all her time doing "tracking stats," writing "line-ups," or glued to some message board discussing the merits of taping make-up sponges to her blisters. Then, when you slump off to the pub to drown your sorrows with your mates, she rolls in two hours after you, red-faced, and laughing about the after-party.

Bargaining: You are a product of the modern age, no? You can handle this if she'll just give in a bit. But your attempts to keep Wednesdays for "us" time and to coax her to take the summer holiday somewhere where she can't visit a local league just aren't making it go away.

Sadness: You miss her. It's common to experience "What if" questions at this stage, like "What if I had just encouraged her to join something more delicate, like street fighting or kendo instead?"

Acceptance: Hard as it may be to understand this, you will eventually learn to embrace your roller derby girl. You may start to realize that your mates crowd around with anticipation to hear about the latest pile-up at practice; that when you finally watch a bout it feels like your first rock concert; or that you've tried on the referee stripes and have developed a taste of your own for the track. The women of the roller derby are a rare breed who will find the derby with or without you. All you can do is thank the derby goddesses above, and start on that sign for the next bout.

NINTH COMMANDMENT:
SAY HELLO TO YOUR NEW FAMILY.

PHOTO BY MARC "STALKERAZZI" CAMPOS

goodie two skates
of team awesome

One of the most rewarding and the most challenging things about becoming part of a league and of the sport on a broader level is that you suddenly gain an international network of people who are more than willing to bail you out of emotional distress, medical hardships, even jail, without hesitation.

Skaters injured in the line of duty have consistently been overwhelmed by the outpouring of financial and physical support provided by sisters in the sport that they've never even met in person. A bevy of babysitters are at the ready to provide track-side childcare for all the derby spawn. Going to Boston this summer? Dial up the Boston Derby Dames, and ten to one says you'll find a couch for the duration. Rollergirls love to support one another through good and bad times. It is a community filled with a wave of mutual respect and admiration. Most of the time.

But the stifling feeling of family can also arise. Keep in mind that you are now regularly required to cooperate with a league full of women who you sometimes see more in a week than you do your actual family.

AM I A DERBY GIRL?

131

We probably don't have to tell you what kind of disagreements and stand-offs can sometimes result from this hormonal proximity. You may have chosen to be a part of this derby brood, but that doesn't necessarily mean you'll get along with everyone, and vice versa. There will, undoubtedly, be a few girls that drive you up a tree on a regular basis. After all, how ludicrous is it to expect women in a sport that regularly attracts hardheaded, empowered rebels to always play nice? There's phrase for that in this industry. It's called **derby drama**—and there's plenty of it. Sometimes arguments over something as inane as the choice of bout intro songs can become so heated that you'll wake up days later painfully embarrassed at your own obsessive vehemence. But occasionally, on the track, even those whose personalities repel you might earn your begrudging respect for their blocking or jamming skills.

TENTH COMMANDMENT:
EVEN THE AFTER-PARTIES HAVE WINNERS.

After the adrenaline tsunami of a hard-fought, scrappy bout there is nothing like a good raucous after-party to stave off the feeling that you've just gotten beaten like a dime store piñata. But if you think for one minute that the competition stays on the track, you are dead wrong.

Dance-offs, drinking battles, kissing contests, and ill-advised feats of strength are just a few of the creative ways rollergirls love to shock innocent bystanders with competitive post-game shenanigans. In fact, it's widely known in the sport that a large amount of injuries are experienced during moments of after-party jackass-ery. Did we mention that we get kicked out of bars . . . a lot?

Humming from the violence of the night's games, skaters often like to stretch the night well into the morning, reliving war stories and making nice with the opponents that were their bitter rivals only hours before. Although there is definitely a contingent of skaters who embrace moderation or sobriety, there are also a slew of rollergirls who drink as skillfully as they skate. In the morning, you are likely to hear several of the members of the defeated squad claiming that they "may have lost the game, but totally won the after-party."

SO, ARE YOU A DERBY GIRL?

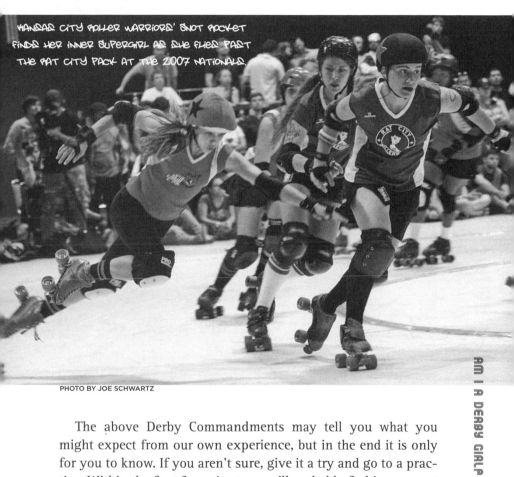

KANSAS CITY ROLLER WARRIORS' SNOT ROCKET FINDS HER INNER SUPERGIRL AS SHE FLIES PAST THE RAT CITY PACK AT THE 2007 NATIONALS.

PHOTO BY JOE SCHWARTZ

The above Derby Commandments may tell you what you might expect from our own experience, but in the end it is only for you to know. If you aren't sure, give it a try and go to a practice. Within the first few minutes you'll probably feel in your gut whether this is the right thing for you. Besides, what's the worst that could happen? Well, you could break your leg . . . but you could also find your true calling. As we see it, the odds are worth playing.

Before you run out and pillage your local skate shop, read the next chapter. It will give you all the tools of the trade, tips, and fun facts to get you rolling in your first jam.

TIME OUT!
Miss Moxxxie's Tips for Winning the After-party

THE B.A.D. GIRLS CHANNEL THE GOLDEN GIRLS . . . AND PLENTY OF LONE STAR BEER

PHOTO BY RICK MARR

DISCLAIMER: HERCULEAN DRINKING FEATS, pantsless dance contests, and bar-top chicken fights are not permitted during games, but they often find a way to infuse after-parties with a little extra holy in their shit.

Skaters such as Betty Ford Galaxy from the Rat City Rollers in Seattle, who has been sober for more than seven years, can tell you that after-parties are wild with or without the booze. "I am often the craziest one at a party or event so a lot of people just assume I drink or

DOWN AND DERBY

something, but nope," she says. It's all about the company and the release after a game.

Or, if you're one of the Bay Area Derby Girls from San Francisco, California, who refuse to politely pack their competitive natures away with their gear after the bout is over, it's all about winning. Whether they win or lose on the track, their after-party record proudly remains undefeated.

But how, exactly, does one "win" an after-party? Miss Moxxxie, longtime B.A.D. Girls member and co-founder of *HELLARAD*, the premiere derby lifestyle 'zine, provides the following five basic tips:

1. **Show up. No matter what.**
   Obviously, you can't win an after-party if you don't go. I remember in 2008 after getting pummeled by the Texas Rollergirls at WFTDA Western Regionals, a lot of us B.A.D. Girls were really bummin' and didn't even want to show our faces at that after-party. But we put on our best black and gold, threw back a couple shots of Kentucky's finest, and made our way out anyway. What do you know? It was a pretty damn good night.

2. **Include the After-party in Your Team's Strategy.**
   You totally rule at knowing when to call off the jam. You've had meetings specifically about the loopholes in the latest rule set and how to use them to your team's advantage. But seriously, leave a little time to chat about what your team is going to wear/do/yell at the after-party that will totally take it to the next level.

3. **Enter as a Team, Leave as a Team.**
   Nobody's going to bat an eye if your girls straggle in two at a titme, go to opposite corners of the bar and sit quietly with their beers. Roll deep. Coordinate a

grand entrance with your entire team, all at once, and stick together on that dance floor! Leave no teammate behind!

4. **Endurance.**

Just as important during the after-party as it is the game. You don't quit at the halftime, you skate your ass off 'till that very last whistle! Don't leave the after-party until the bar is kicking you out. And remember, there's always time for an after-after-party (houses with hot tubs are strongly encouraged). We learned our after-party endurance from the L.A. Derby Dolls who have a puritan work ethic in this area. They go so far as to meet up the next morning for a Bloody Mary/burrito breakfast that lasts until the following evening.

5. **All for One, One for All.**

More than anything, the after-party is a chance to show everyone how much team spirit you have. So naturally, your entire team has to be on board with the "theme" and be willing to take it as far as humanly possible to ensure victory. You've got your jammers back in the pack, don't leave her hanging when she's shakin' it on the pool table.

But if you're still wondering what a winning after-party strategy might entail, Miss Moxxxie happily recounts the following September 2009 B.A.D. Girls victory:

The #16 ranked B.A.D. Girls traveled to Austin for a bout with the #2 Texas Rollergirls Texecutioners, and we heard there was some sort of trophy up for grabs for the winners of the after-party. In true Bay Area style, we were not about to take that shit lightly.

We were in high spirits, especially after our traditional half hour of power drinking in the parking lot. In a choreographed wave of black and gold, the Bay Area Derby Girls entered the bar dressed in full sparkly Golden Girl grandma gear, sporting gray wigs, sequined dresses, and hella bronzer. The DJ took a hint and blared "Golddigger" as we mobbed the place, dancing through a cheering crowd of Texans and stunned Texecutioners, kicking people off pool tables where games were in progress so we could dance on top of them. Lone Star tall cans were handed our way, sweaty people got nearly naked, and wig-switching ensued.

Texas tried to rally with some weak ass cheerleader shit. But they were stopped in their tracks when the DJ put on Rick James' "Superfreak" and our Jheri-Curl-wigged Belle "Right" Hooks lost her mind on the dance floor.

We were rightfully awarded the after-party trophy, and celebrated our win with street corner hot dogs and more beer (passengers can drink legally in Texas) on the ride home.

Moral of the story: Don't challenge the B.A.D. Girls to an after-party unless you are prepared to lose your shirt. Literally.

I AM A DERBY GIRL!

CONGRATULATIONS! YOU'VE DECIDED you want to give roller derby a whirl . . . So now what do you do? Just as this sport welcomes women of all shapes and types, there is no one-size-fits-all approach to playing roller derby either. Thousands of women have joined the world of derby and evolved within it, each in her own way. That's one of the things we love about this sport, no two derby career paths are alike.

That said, there are certain steps that sooner or later you're bound to take. So, without further ado, here's our 12-Step Program for life as a derby girl!

1. FIND A LEAGUE.

One of the first things you'll want to do is find a league with which you can skate. The term "league" usually refers to a group of people committed to playing roller derby. Beyond that, no two leagues are exactly alike. Some are just starting up with no more than a dozen or so women who are learning the basics of skating. Other leagues have been around for years, each with more than a hundred members, established teams, and a venue where bouts are regularly held.

If you're in a major metropolis or even a midsized 'burb, do a quick online search and you'll likely find a league nearby. From the Rage City Rollergirls in Anchorage, Alaska, to the Beach Brawl Sk8R Dolls of Destin, Florida, there are hundreds of leagues throughout the U.S.—and several dozen more around the world.

Most leagues have a website or MySpace profile that provides information on how to join or contacts so you can drop the league a line and find out what you need to know to enroll. First and foremost, if you are under twenty-one years old, ask about the league's age requirement. For a number of reasons, including safety and insurance, many leagues require participating skaters be at least twenty-one or eighteen years old. If you're not, don't despair—lots of leagues have Junior Derby for younger girls. Otherwise, we suggest you start counting down the days until your birthday and spend as many of them skating as you can!

Some derby leagues will let you join any time of year you like. This is especially true of newer leagues looking to build up a solid roster of skaters. Leagues that have been around for a while may not be in need of as many new recruits. They may offer tryouts or introductory sessions only at certain times of their season. If this is the case in your town and you just missed tryouts, we recommend you take advantage of the downtime and spend as much of it on eight wheels as you can. And be sure to stay in touch so you know when you will next be able to try out or join.

If you're living in places such as Los Angeles, Indianapolis, or Bend, Oregon, you may find yourself with some choices to make. These cities, and quite a few others, are currently home to more than one league. Sometimes, multiple leagues in one town get along just fine, in other cases the relationships are . . . shall we say, a bit delicate. So, before you go out and get that new league tattoo on your forearm, we suggest you do a bit of research and make sure you're choosing the league that's right for you.

Find out about each of the leagues and what makes them different. Do they skate banked or flat track? Who runs the league? What is their league mission? What rules do they use? If the league was once part of another league, finding out why they split might be a sensitive, but worthwhile line of questioning.

Most importantly, get to know the people involved. Remember, you will be spending a *lot* of time with these folks, so you want to be sure they're ones you get along with or at least can pretty well tolerate for several hours a week without wanting to cram your wrist guards down their throats.

Finally, perhaps you're desperate to join derby but you live in Glendive, Montana; or Eustis, Maine; or Kumamoto, Japan. You may find yourself in a derby-free zone, but don't give up hope! You can always start up your own league. Yes, it will take a huge amount of time, effort, and patience, but it's been done before. Just think about how much joy you could bring to potential derby girls in your neck of the woods!

We're not going to get into the details of how to start your own league here (that could easily fill a whole other book!). But know this—there are plenty of women out there who've started a league from scratch. Most of them will be happy to offer advice and guidance about how to get rolling in your town. After all, the more leagues in existence, the more opportunities there are for competition and travel!

2. GET YOUR GEAR.

Roller derby is a violent contact sport and injury is, to a certain degree, inevitable. That said, we do our best to protect ourselves and, fortunately, there's some great gear out there to help you do that. So let's take it from the top . . .

Helmet

Derby skaters use the same sorts of helmets most skateboarders use with a hard outer shell, foam on the inside, and straps that fasten under your chin. Yes, there are some really cool-looking ones on the market in adorable bubblegum pink or badass camo patterns, but do yourself and your noggin a huge favor. Go for the helmet that fits the best, not the one that looks the coolest. Make sure to adjust the straps so the helmet fits snugly. A head is a terrible thing to waste!

Mouth Guard

You can find mouth guards at most sporting goods stores (try looking in the football section). Mouth guards are rounded pieces of plastic that fit over your teeth to prevent them from being knocked out of your mouth (yes, it happens—ask our dear friend Iron Maiven!).

Cheap mouth guards will cost you a couple of bucks, but you get what you pay for. Many ladies complain that these do-'em-yourself mouth guards are uncomfortable and gag-inducing. If you agree, you might want to consider having a custom mouth guard made by your dentist. It will cost you a fair bit more, but the ability to skate without projectile vomiting will be well worth it. And the dentist can often whip up a mouth guard in your team or league colors!

We recommend getting a case for your mouth guard—it will help keep the mouth guard free of nasty sock fuzz and track dust. Plus, a case will make it easier to find when you're digging around in your gear bag. We also advise occasionally soaking your mouth guard in mouthwash or rinse to keep it tasty and germ-free.

A MONTREAL ROLLER DERBY GIRL SPORTS HER MOUTH GUARD

Elbow Pads, Knee Pads, and Wrist Guards

This is the Holy Trinity of protective gear—the items you absolutely cannot do without. You'll find they come in plenty of different styles, shapes, and colors (though black is predominant). Again, make sure they fit you well and don't just look good.

Putting elbow and knee pads on for the first time may be a

bit intimidating, and strapping them on upside down is a telltale sign of a skating neophyte. Here's a hint: most pads have a piece of plastic on the front with one edge curved; this curve should be at the top of your elbow or knee.

Like the rest of your gear, you can get cheap pads and wrist guards, which may not be a bad idea at first, if you are not entirely convinced you're ready to become a full-time derby girl. But if you stick with the sport, there's a good chance you'll want to invest a bit more in serious equipment. Some companies will even design a pair of custom pads or wrist guards for you if you send them your measurements.

Butt Pads

Did you ever imagine you'd take on a hobby involving armor for your ass? Bet not. Butt pads are not usually a required purchase for doing derby in the same way that the gear mentioned above is, but they're a very worthwhile investment. Butt pads look like bicycle shorts with a lot of padding built in, especially around the hips and tailbone. Pull on a pair and you will likely look like the love child of the Michelin Tire man and Darth Vader. But trust us, when you take that first hard fall on your ass, you will be incredibly thankful for that extra cushion.

Shin Guards

Again, not required, but strongly recommended. Though you don't fall on your shins that often in derby, skaters often kick upward when they stride, and when someone else's wheels smack into your shinbones it smarts something fierce. Shin guards can help protect you from that. Of course, they also add to that overall modern day gladiator look. And did we mention they come in silver, pink, or with flames racing up the front?

Goggles

If you have a nice pair of glasses, we strongly advise you *not* to wear them when doing roller derby. Technically speaking, most leagues will not allow hits to the face. But that doesn't mean it never hap-

ANATOMY OF A ROLLERGIRL

HELMET

MOUTH GUARD
(stays tasty tucked in bra)

ELBOW PAD

WRIST GUARD

KNEE PADS

QUAD SPEED SKATES

MÖTLEY CRÜZ OF THE BAY AREA DERBY GIRLS MODELS GEAR PROVIDED BY CRUZSKATESHOP.COM

pens. Most gals with vision issues opt for contact lenses or sport goggles. Remember, safety is sexy. Or at least it beats blindness.

You can find all of the above items online; be sure to compare prices to make sure you're getting the best deal. But we also strongly advise you try on a non-virtual version of whatever you're buying online first. Ask someone in your league of similar proportions to make sure you are getting the best size and style for you.

3. GET YOUR SKATES.

And now we've come to the good stuff—your roller skates! Modern day derby girls skate on quad skates. Quads are roller skates with two wheels in the front and two in the back. These are different from in-line skates with wheels arranged in a single line.

If you are not one hundred percent certain this sport is for you, you may first want to see if your league has some extra pairs of skates lying around that you can borrow. Or, if your league practices at a rink, they'll probably have skates you can rent.

Skating on borrowed wheels should be able to give you enough of a taste of roller derby to know whether or not you plan to stick with it. If so, we suggest getting yourself a decent pair of your own. These skates should prove more comfortable. You'll be the only one wearing them, so they'll eventually mold to fit like your favorite pair of jeans.

The four main components of quad roller skates are: boots, plates, wheels, and bearings. The **boot** is the main, shoe-like part of the skate. Be sure to invest in something that fits well. Most boots have a breaking in period—an inglorious time of blisters and frustration. You want to make sure once you come out of those miserable woods that your boots fit you like a pair of comfy slippers. To further the cozy factor, we recommend replacing the insole on your skates with a nice pair of cushioned or athletic insoles, available at most drug stores.

Plates are the pieces that connect the boots to the wheels. They are usually made out of nylon or aluminum. There is a wide range of price when it comes to plates. It's definitely worth investing some money in since cheap plates have been known to snap with the rigors of derby. But does this mean you need the ritzy Italian aluminum plates that cost more than your first car did? Probably not.

Wheels are like ice cream . . . or sex toys. They are colorful and come in all sorts of different kinds. Finding the ones you like best is largely a matter of taste and something to be discovered through experimentation, but oh, what a fun thing to test!

There are two main types of wheels—indoor and outdoor wheels. If you can afford it, it's a good idea to invest in a pair of each. Indoor wheels are best suited for banked tracks and the slick floors found in many flat-track venues. Outdoor wheels have a lot more shock absorption and will come in handy if you skate on parking lots, streets, and sidewalks, where surfaces are less smooth and prone to cracks.

Bearings are small antifriction devices that fit inside your skate wheels and serve as a buffer between them and the axle attached to your plate. Skate bearings look like small, flat metal donuts. Bearings can be purchased quite inexpensively . . . or you can invest a nice chunk of your paycheck in a set. Again, we advise you to ask around, do some research, and experiment to see what works best for you. Also, be sure to order the right size—most skates are designed with eight millimeter axles, but some use seven millimeter, and you'll need to get the appropriate bearing size.

Now, a word about **toe-stops**. If you skated at all as a kid, there's a good chance you used skates with stoppers—those big rubber plugs in the front of the skate. Lots of derby girls use toe-stops. Many find them helpful for quick take-offs and fancy backward stops. Others prefer not to use toe-stops, relying instead on the strength and skill of their own legs to slow them down. In this case, you'll likely want to opt for something known as a toe plug. These small pieces of rubber screw into the front end of your plate to make sure it doesn't scrape the floor.

If all this shopping seems a bit daunting, take some comfort in knowing many companies offer skate packages with pre-selected boots, plates, wheels, and bearings. Especially when you're first getting started, these packages can be a convenient option. Most skate shops also let you build your own roller skates with your choice of boot, plate, bearings, and wheels—definitely the way to go for the more discerning skater.

As you mull over these decisions, there are some basic questions you'll want to consider. What type of surface will you be

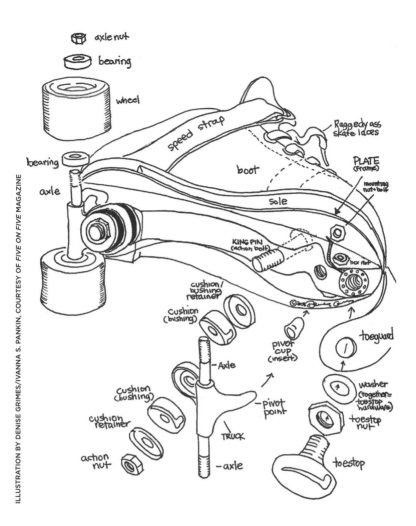

ILLUSTRATION BY DENISE GRIMES/IVANNA S. PANKIN, COURTESY OF FIVE ON FIVE MAGAZINE

skating on most often? How big are you? Do you prefer getting as much speed as possible, or are you more of a controlled skater when it comes to pace? Are you okay with leather? And if the answer to that last one is no, don't worry, there are plenty of great vegan skates on the market, too!

Your local roller skating rink probably has a shop and, hopefully, someone working there will be knowledgeable and friendly enough to guide you. Also, ask around in your league; see what skates and wheels other girls like. And finally, there are a number of great skate companies out there with an expert staff. Derby girls who can offer insider advice own several of these shops. Don't be afraid to ask questions, try skates on, and make sure you are making a selection you believe in before you lay down the cash.

Now that roller derby has been around for a while, a number of companies also offer rookie packages that come complete with helmet, pads, and a solid pair of beginner skates. These packages offer a great way to get all your gear at once and, usually, at a good discount.

Another option is buying used. After all, in the great circle of derby life, skaters retire and when they do, some of them sell their gear. If you can deal with someone else's stink, you can certainly save. Other times skaters buy gear, realize it doesn't work for them, and offer up items that are barely worn for a good discount. You can often find what you are looking for on derby message boards and online auction sites.

Finally, there are some skate accessories you may want to purchase. First up is a **skate tool.** This is a piece of equipment that will help you loosen or tighten your trucks and wheels, remove and install your bearings, and make other little adjustments on the fly. Though most derby practice venues will have a skate tool you can use, it's nice to have one of your own, especially to use when you're skating outside of practice. Also, you may want to pick up bearing cleaner and lube to keep your bearings in good shape. You'll find both online and at skate shops.

Of course you'll need something to put all of this gear in—rollergirls use everything from duffle bags to metal box cases and rolling suitcases. There are now even skate bags specifically designed with the competing derby girl in mind! Our only piece of advice here—don't leave your skate bag in your car. Seriously. It's so tempting to leave that heavy bag of stinky stuff out of the house, but we cannot begin to tell you how many rollergirls have lost their gear to thieves—a true heartbreak!

PROFiLE: Ivanna S. Pankin and Trish the Dish

Before roller derby, Ivanna S. Pankin was a married punk rock chick looking for something more in life. Trish the Dish was a former athlete, bored and stuck in a depressing cubicle job.

That was then. This is now.

Today, Ivanna and Trish are the power couple of roller derby—they've been together much longer than most leagues have been in existence. Ivanna, as you recall, was the founder of the Arizona Roller Derby (AZRD) league. Together the two went on to start Sin City Rollergirls in Las Vegas, where they skated for two years before moving to California and joining the San Diego Derby Dolls in 2009. They're also the founders of Sin City Skates—a skate shop just for derby girls.

Q: *What did you two think of each other when you first met?*

IVANNA S. PANKIN: I thought Dish hated me because she was always staring. She inspired me because she was aggressive even before she learned how to skate at all. She would cling to the wall in between trying to fling herself at people. And she led her team to play strategically, while my team leaned on the strengths of individual players. She provided the next and most interesting step in the game for me—strategy and teamwork.

TRISH THE DISH: We were rival captains, so we didn't do much socializing with each other. Back then, it was all about the home teams, so people looked at you odd if they caught you talking to an opponent. About halfway through the season, I started to do the Bout Management, and we got to know each other pretty well because of the workload.

Q: *In 2005, you two started Sin City Skates. How did that come about?*

IS: A rep from the Sure Grip skate company came out to visit a team practice when she was in Vegas visiting her mother. I approached her to sponsor our league, and asked if we could use our resale license to get wholesale gear for our skaters. She told me that they only way Sure Grip could sell wholesale to us was if we had a skate shop that sold to other people besides our team. Coincidentally, I was incredibly underemployed as a temp worker at the time, so the idea sounded pretty good to me. I created the website during Christmastime, figuring I'd do it until I got a "real" job or until orders dried up after Christmas. They still haven't.

Q: *What strengths do you think each of you brings to your partnership?*

TD: Ivanna is the creator. She is so intelligent and artistic, but she also knows how to make those dreams happen. I think I am the maintainer; I am a workhorse, and help her keep all of her projects moving forward.

IS: Dish has tons of sports experience. She is an incredibly hard worker and a patient person. Between the two of us, we are more than the sum of our parts.

Q: What are the benefits and challenges of owning a derby-related business?

TD: The benefits are obvious, we don't miss derby events that we want to see, and we know thousands of derby girls around the world. This is the best job I've ever had. The challenges? I like challenges.

Q: You live together, you run a business together, you two spend a lot of time together. So what's it like when you skate together on a team?

TD: When we play together, it is almost like we are just extensions of each other.

IS: We have figured out game strengths that are complementary, so we play better together. We just recently started trying to switch, actually, because our bodies are getting so fucked up. We figure if we learn each other's specialties and hits, we'll have another six or seven years until the other halves of our bodies are equally fucked up.

Q: What's it like in situations where you skate against each other?

TD: Usually everything is good for a while, but then we both start getting really passionate and we usually start calling each other's fouls and things.

Q: Do you think you'll ever retire?

IS: Of course. My body can only take so much abuse. I'll retire when I start sucking or I feel like I'm not getting any better. It was close this summer . . . I had a string of injuries and lots of doubts. But now I'm feeling fine, so hopefully not too soon!

TD: We all have to retire sometime, maybe when I'm stricken to a wheelchair. Did someone say Wheelchair Derby?

4. GO TO A PRACTICE.

Once you've found a league to skate with and gear to skate in, you are ready for your first practice!

Get in touch with your local league and find out when the next practice is that *you* are able to attend. Bear in mind that many leagues have practices several times a week, but those might only be open to veteran skaters. You are a skater tot, a rinky-dink . . . you are fresh meat!

What's fresh meat, you ask? Basically this is a friendly way to describe women who are learning the ropes of derby and, like nice cuts of raw porterhouse, they're about to be tenderized!

As fresh meat, it's your job to find out what your league recommends bringing to your first practice. This could include a bottle of something to keep hydrated, gear, and maybe some cash or a check to pay for practice. This fee helps the league pay for its practice space and put on bouts. If you're a sweaty Betty, you'll probably want to bring a towel, too.

Wear comfortable clothes. Though we get dolled up for public bouts, practice is not a time for dressing to impress. You'll want to wear something you can easily move around in but nothing so baggy that it could get caught up in someone else's wheels should you fall. If you have long hair, you might want to bring something to tie it back with—nothing sucks more than not seeing a hit coming because your tresses got in the way!

Show up to practice early. Yeah, this is a hobby, and we skate primarily for fun, but we take derby seriously. Showing up late, especially at your first practice, is unwise and, frankly, rude to others, especially your trainer.

Introduce yourself. There's a good chance someone will be at practice to welcome you, but it's always nice to show a bit of initiative. Remember, we knock each other out on the track, but we don't bite (it's illegal under the current rules). Most skaters will be happy to see a new face. After all, at some point, we were all fresh meat, too, just like you.

A league representative or trainer for the evening may well have you fill out some forms and sign some releases (another reason to show up early)! If you have any pre-existing medical conditions or injuries, please share them with the coach or trainer in advance. He or she will want to know if you are recently recovering from a twisted ankle or pinched nerve. The trainer can help you adjust accordingly so as not to hurt yourself (any more than necessary, that is).

Finally, if you are on the shy side, keep an eye out for fellow fresh meat. It's nice to know there are others in the same awkward boat. Any journey worth taking is better with a friend. Who knows? Your first derby buddy might end up being your derby wife.

TRAINING IN ROCHESTER, NEW YORK, WITH THE ROC CITY ROLLER DERBY

5. CHOOSE YOUR DERBY NAME.

So you made it through your first few practices. You've got blisters the size of your thumbs and shin splints that make you whimper at work, but you can already tell you're smitten with the sport. In that case, it might be time to start thinking about your derby name. Your derby name is a crucial part of your skating persona. For girls in occupations that might frown on derby, derby names also provide an excellent cover.

Picking your derby nom du guerre is like choosing your first tattoo. You want one that means something to you, not something you pick arbitrarily on a drinking jag in Tijuana. The last thing you want is to wake up one morning, look in the mirror, and think, "Holy crap, what was I thinking?" Because like a tattoo, a skater name is much easier to get than it is to remove.

And once you have it, you'll need to make it a part of you, learning to respond to your derby name as if it were the one printed on your birth certificate. And that can be a bit tricky at first. That's why the woman known in real life as Dallas Parsons took on the name Derby Does Dallas when she joined the Dutchland Rollers of Pennsylvania.

Dallas isn't the only one to play off her real name. Leigh Pinney of the Rage City Rollergirls in Anchorage, Alaska, says she might not be the fastest jammer or the biggest blocker, but "I hang in there until I get the job done!" That and her love of Jack Black made the name Tenacious-Leigh a perfect fit.

Kat Almond who started doing derby with the Jet City Roller Girls in Everett, Washington, played off her first name to become Kat Ekizm, as in catechism, or Catholic study. The name served her especially well when she moved to Idaho and the Treasure Valley Rollergirls drafted her to the Devil's Darlings team!

Some skaters go for names that cleverly play on words. Try reading these ones aloud—Albie Damned (Renegade Rollergirls), Athena DeCrime (Windy City Rollers), Ima Handful (Rat City Rollergirls), Lotta Trouble (Bleeding Heartland Roller Girls), Pia Mess (Silicon Valley Rollergirls), and Rhoda Badcheck (River City Rollergirls).

Other skaters like to pay tribute to figures in history, cultural heroes, fictional characters, and modern day celebrities. There's Amelia Scareheart (Atlanta Rollergirls), Lois Slain (DC Rollergirls), Billie Midol (Alamo City Rollergirls), Bone Crawford (Jersey

Shore Roller Girls), Tina Turn-her (Sheffield Steel Roller Girls), and Yoko Oh No You Didn't (Pueblo Derby Devil Dollz).

Sometimes skaters like to evoke a quality of their personality. Krista Kay Williams, for instance, is one of the original Rat City Rollergirls, now skating for the Throttle Rockets team. Krista doesn't drink. As she told us, "I am sober and that is a huge part of my life and who I am. I wanted my skate name to reflect that—but not only that," Krista explains. She also wanted something that went with her space-themed team and that invoked her love of old cars. So she opted for Betty Ford Galaxy—classic!

And then of course there's us. Jenny loves movies as much as she loves roller derby. She especially loves it when the two combine! *Kansas City Bomber* is a kitschy roller derby movie starring Raquel Welch. Of course KC are Kansas City's initials—say it aloud and you have Kasey. Hence, Kasey Bomber—a very fitting name for a film buff with a passion for skating.

Alex is a journalist who owns a 1958 Edsel. For her, the name Axles of Evil was a natural fit—it played off "axis of evil"—a term that's earned its place in news history. The name was also a nod to her vintage vehicle; and finally, it played off the letters in her real name—voila!

When it comes to derby names, the possibilities are endless . . . sort of. The great thing about this sport flourishing around the world is that there are thousands of amazing names out there to awe and inspire you. The downside though, is that there are now much fewer names up for grabs.

In the world of roller derby, imitation isn't a form of flattery; it's an invitation to an ass kicking. This is one of the few rules we seem to universally agree on—you can't take another skater's name, even if she lives thousands of miles away.

How do you know your dream name isn't already taken? Thanks to the extracurricular efforts of a few tremendously dedicated skaters, there is a Master Roster in place that helps keep track of which names are being used and by whom.

Back in November 2004, Axles suggested to the then-fledgling derby community that a Master Roster be kept online. Turns out,

Hydra, of the Texas Rollergirls, had already started a spreadsheet of all the flat track skater names. She was wise enough to predict that eventually leagues from different parts of the country would be competing with one another and how mightily confusing it would be to hear an announcer say, "And up next, we have Dee Struction jamming against . . . Dee Struction!"

Hydra set up a Master Roster of skater names that you can now find online at twoevils.org/rollergirls. The list is currently maintained by Paige Burner and Soylent Mean, who dutifully wade through thousands of e-mails each week.

Paige and Soylent have set up some guidelines. First and most obvious rule is no exact duplications. So don't even think about sending in Paige Burner or Soylent Mean. It won't fly.

Names that are spelled or pronounced similarly—for example Page Burner or Paige Burna—will only be accepted if you have *written* permission from the skater with the original name. You also can't choose anything too generic—you can't apply for names like *Skater* or *Rollergirl*. It's just too confusing since we already use those words way too often.

In addition you can't choose names starting with possessives, such as Her Bad Day or Your Worst Nightmare, and no ending with a gerund. That is, you're fine with Speed Skater but not Speed Skating. Such names would make an announcer's job nearly impossible and would confuse audiences. As Soylent Mean explains, can you imagine hearing: "Due to a strong defensive, you can see Caught Speeding slowing down behind the front two blockers . . ."

Finally, most leagues will require that you skate a certain number of practices before submitting your new identity for admission to the Master Roster. After all, what a shame it would be to have a girl take a great name only to ditch derby a few days later! You can submit your choice of name for consideration through a designated league representative once you've met your league's specific requirements.

To date, there are more than 19,500 names registered on the Master Roster, so you may have a tough time finding a name that hasn't been taken. But don't let it get you down. Choosing a skater name can and should be a fun adventure. Enlist the help of your family and friends. Start a list and ask those who know you well to vote on their favorite one. Envision fans at a bout holding up a sign for you and see which name plays out best in that fantasy!

PHOTO BY JULES DOYLE

PHOTO BY JULES DOYLE

TIME OUT!

LEGIT VS. DERBY NAMES

WHEN THIS LATEST INCARNATION of derby got rolling in Austin, the women of Bad Girl, Good Woman decided early on that they would take on skater names that were distinctly different from their real names. "We thought we should be larger than life," recalls original She-E-O April Ritzenthaler. "Naming yourself gave you that extra inspiration to fill out that character."

April eventually became known as La Muerta, but the first derby name she chose was Queen Destroyer—a moniker to go with her fierce new derby persona. "April couldn't be a face-stomping, choking grabber, but Queen Destroyer could!"

Faux names also come in handy for those skaters who, for professional or other reasons, don't want their real

I AM A DERBY GIRL!

157

names associated with a violent sport like derby. But some women enjoy playing derby while using their real names. That's just what a number of skaters from around the country did when they formed Team Legit.

Team Legit member Robyn Baroh (who goes by Rebel Belle when she plays with Rat City) says skating with her real name makes it feel more like a professional sport. "Instead of a persona, it is one hundred percent you," Robyn explains.

But, it can be a little awkward skating with your real name if you're used to being called by a derby name. Robyn says Team Legit tried to use real names whenever they hung out together. "The transition wasn't quite smooth," says Robyn, "I would yell 'Sheeza, oh wait . . . Katie!' a lot at first."

Every now and then, skaters have proposed using real names on a more regular basis. Some argue that roller derby would have a better chance of being taken seriously as a sport if we skated under our real names. After all, it is easier to imagine the International Olympic Committee accepting a sport featuring an athlete named Wendi Wentzell than one named Kat Von D'Stroya.

But most rollergirls believe that derby names are here to stay. "We still continue to make the public take us seriously on our own terms—by playing a great sport and working hard on the track," says Kristin "Mercy Less" Seale of the Charm City Roller Girls. "Choosing our own names is a big part of our culture that won't disappear any time soon, and is a time honored sports tradition—from Babe Ruth to Ocho Cinco."

6. CHOOSE A SKATE NUMBER.

Luckily, choosing a number is *way* easier than choosing a name. Most leagues are fairly flexible about numbers. Usually as long as it's not a number already taken by a skater within your league, you're good to go.

Again this is an opportunity to chose a number that means something to you. Axles chose #58 because that's the year of her Edsel. Kasey opted for #72 because that's the year *Kansas City Bomber* premiered.

Also keep in mind that we use the term "number" very loosely. Some skaters continue the fun of their name with the number that appears below it on their jerseys. Aimzz 2 Kill of the Atlanta Rollergirls is "20/20." Ali Mony of TXRD Lonestar Rollergirls is "$10,000 a month." Baberaham Lincoln of the Brewcity Bruisers is "4 score 7 beers ago." Xero Tolerance of Sisters of Mayhem Roller Girls is "101 proof." And Herrah Tic of the Omaha Roller-girls is darn near Satanic at "665.9"!

7. GET INVOLVED.

Roller derby leagues aren't run by magical gnomes. They're only able to operate thanks to the hard work of skaters. Most leagues have a board and/or a group of committees tasked with various responsibilities. The organization of a league varies from place to place, but we'd be pretty shocked if your league wouldn't welcome you volunteering some of your time off-skates.

Are you a web design whiz? You might be able to help create or maintain your league's website. Do you have a background in accounting? You can lend a hand with league finances. Have a penchant for cooking? Maybe you can organize a fundraising bake sale. Are you well-organized and great at taking notes? You could be your league's next Secretary of Skate!

The opportunities are endless, and there is always a way to

help, even if it's just taking out the trash at the end of practice. Check with vets in your league to see what assistance is needed and how you can contribute. Lending a helping hand will definitely be appreciated by your league-mates.

Note that putting in some extra time may not be a voluntary choice. Often times, league members are required to put in hours supervising the parking lot, selling merchandise, or taking tickets at bouts.

Working is often the less glamorous, more tedious side of derby. Cleaning up human feces from the side of the track and emptying out stale cans of beer was not exactly what we envisioned when we first enlisted. Once, fellow Derby Doll Trixie Biscuit removed a goat carcass from the parking lot (don't ask how it got there—nobody knows)! But, you gotta do what you gotta do.

Helping out your league off-skates can also be fun. It's a great opportunity to learn more about your fellow skaters and what they're capable of doing. It can also be a chance to learn some

A BIG EASY ROLLERGIRL HELPS CLEAN UP.

PHOTO BY KERRY MCCLAIN

new skills for free. Who knows? Derby may be the beginning of a new career. That's what Lorna Boom and Hurt Reynolds of Rat City Rollergirls did when they teamed up with Mercy Less of Duke City Derby to start Have Derby Will Travel in the summer of 2009. The three of them used the skills they honed starting and running roller derby leagues to launch a full-service consulting firm for non-profits and for-profit grassroots businesses.

"Derby gives you a platform to take all of your best strengths and use them for something you really care about," says Mercy Less, who also served as WFTDA treasurer. "I had never been the treasurer of an organization, and finance was certainly not my department. But with derby, there are all these trial by fire opportunities to learn."

8. GET CONNECTED.

Want to know when your practices are, how to reach fellow league members, when your coach's birthday is, or where everyone is getting together on Friday night? There's a good chance all this information and more exists somewhere online. Most leagues have an online group that helps everyone stay informed and connected. A lot of us use Yahoo or Google groups. These groups are places to find information like rules, everyone's contact information, or links to local skate shops. They're great places to get advice on everything from the local chiropractor to which skates are best for your venue.

You may find that your fellow league members are also a fantastic resource for things that have nothing to do with skating. Need a good plumber, someone to look after your cat for a few days, a new drummer for your band? Derby girls are there for one another and can be a superb support group.

There are usually several online groups for different teams, committees, etc. There will likely be some rules about who can join which groups and some basic etiquette to follow. *Don't* vent your frustrations about another skater or a ref to the entire group—that's bad form!

Once you've gotten comfortable in your new derby existence, you'll probably want to meet gals from other leagues. If you've got the time and the money, travel is a great way to do this. Going to RollerCon and inter-league tournaments is a fantastic opportunity to meet other skaters.

But you don't need to wait for an inter-league game to take advantage of the tremendous travel opportunities roller derby provides. When skaters head out of town for work or for fun, we usually get in touch with the league(s) in our destination town or city. You can usually find contact information online. Most leagues have a special Inter-league Liaison who is the point person for helping out-of-town visitors.

Dropping in on another league's practice or bout is a great way to learn new skills and make new friends. Many times, with enough advance notice, a league will be more than happy to take you out on the town, and even find you a couch to crash on for a few nights. May we recommend you bring a few buttons and t-shirts from your league to share as a token of your appreciation?

If you can't travel, you can also connect with other rollergirls online. You'll find many skaters maintain a derby presence on social networking sites. Also, there is a Yahoo group for rollergirls at groups.yahoo.com/roller_girls. It has thousands of members, many of whom are there to answer questions and share advice and anecdotes.

TIME OUT!

RollerCon

ROLLERCON, THE ANNUAL ROLLER derby convention, means different things to different people. For some, it's the opportunity to chicken-fight in the pool with girls from other leagues you just met, while drinking a blend of Gatorade and cheap vodka out of a hotel ice bucket. For others, it's skating from dawn to dusk and then some in clinics, challenges, and open scrimmages. For most of us, it's a bit of both.

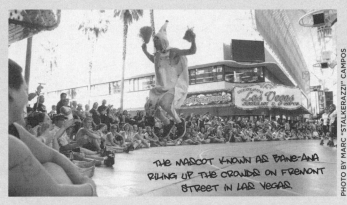

THE MASCOT KNOWN AS BANE-ANA RILING UP THE CROWDS ON FREMONT STREET IN LAS VEGAS.

PHOTO BY MARC "STALKERAZZI" CAMPOS

RollerCon began in the summer of 2005 as a long weekend of scrimmaging and revelry in the ridiculous heat of Las Vegas. The event now draws hundreds of derby folk from as far away as Brisbane, Australia. Each day features a wide array of activities—it takes more than 250 volunteers to make all that skating and socializing possible. Here are a few of the highlights we believe no RollerCon would be complete without:

Seminars: RollerCon features all sorts of clinics and workshops for just about every type of person involved in the sport. For skaters, there are classes on everything from plyometric training and pre-

I AM A DERBY GIRL!

163

workout yoga, to falling for smart people and ninja blocking. For production types, there are seminars on derby bookkeeping, shooting derby video, dealing with controversial ref calls, and finding the right announcer for your league. Who knew a trip to Vegas could be such an educational experience?

Black N' Blue Ball: Named for the bruises we earn on the track, the Black N' Blue Ball is a formal (well, as formal as we get in derby) dance. Folks get dressed to the nines and boogie. One year we danced so hard, they had to shut the ball down early for fear the chandelier was gonna crash down on us.

Out and About: Though most folks spend the bulk of their time at the hotel or at the various skating venues, there are also opportunities to venture out and explore Sin City. There are guided tours of skate parks—a great chance to learn how to vert skate with the pros. The annual RollerCon Scavenger Hunt gives rollergirls a chance to run around Vegas on ridiculous missions such as switching outfits with a showgirl or getting Wayne Newton's autograph.

Derby Wedding: As mentioned previously, each year derby peeps recite vows that join them in holy skating matrimony. Derby weddings have been held in the parking lot of punk rock clubs and in front of the Hogs-N-Heifers Bar (the inspiration for the film *Coyote Ugly*). Tourists on Vegas' Fremont Street are always a bit shocked to see a procession of girls in skates and wedding veils traipsing off to get hitched!

Challenges: Challenges are short mini-bouts featuring teams put together specifically for RollerCon. These are awesome opportunities for hilarious themes and outrageous costumes. For example, RollerCon challenges have pitted Star Trek fans against Star Wars fans, the Itty Bitty Titty

Committee versus Over the Shoulder Boulder Holders, and Ninjas facing off against Pirates.

At RollerCon 2009, the California Regional Association of Players (a.k.a. C*R*A*P) dressed up as lifeguards, complete with zinc on their noses and pool floaties over their elbow pads. They took on a team of skaters from the Pacific Northwest who dressed up as lumberjacks in plaid shirts and fake beards. Each time a lifeguard jammer got out of the pack, she would move her arms as if she was swimming around the track; the lumberjacks would hack with their arms as if they were sawing down the competition.

Open Scrimmages: Ever since the inaugural RollerCon, skaters have brought white and black t-shirts to wear at open scrimmages. These scrimmages are great chances to meet people from other leagues. There's no teams or score keeping, so it's a super fun opportunity to knock around and skate without the pressure of worrying about winning.

Magical Moments: Some of the most memorable times at RollerCon are the ones that aren't planned— singing along with the Michael Jackson impersonator in the hotel lobby or making a new derby friend from London who offers to put you up at her house.

Several folks recall taking the red double-decker bus from the Las Vegas Sports Center back to the Imperial Hotel one night at RollerCon '09. One of the skaters on board spotted a young mother with several children walking along Las Vegas Boulevard. They brought her and her family on board. A Spanish-speaking skater spoke with her and learned that her husband had kicked her out of the car in the middle of nowhere. The derby folks on board the bus passed a helmet around and collected cash to send the family safely on their way!

9. GET STINKY.

You might have noticed at your first practice that there was a certain smell in the air—one that could have made a slaughtered skunk on a summer night in Florida smell like a rose. That's not just the fragrance of your nervous excitement—that's the fine bouquet of roller derby.

Skaters tend to sweat a lot, and that sweat, filled with all sorts of noxious toxins, gets absorbed into protective gear. Derby girls are known to throw their wet, pungent pads back into a skate bag, then leave them zipped up to stew in their own juices for days, even weeks, at a time. Some skaters think of this as a weapon in their arsenal—fend off opponents with the wretched odor emanating from your wrist guards!

But the stench is pretty inexcusable to your non-derby friends and it doesn't come off easily with soap and water either. So we offer these tips on staying funk free.

If nothing else, take your pads out of your bag and let them air and dry out between practices. Trust us, putting on a pair of wet pads is about as pleasant as pulling on a soggy bathing suit on a humid day. You might also want to spritz your gear with some sort of scented anti-microbial spray as you let it dry out.

Wash your gear on a regular basis. You might not be able to do this after every practice and game, but try to do it when you can. Check with the manufacturer of your pads to see what they recommend in terms of cleaning. If your washing machine has a good delicate cycle, you might want to give that a shot, though sometimes that can wear down the Velcro and foam, or break down the fabric.

Other methods skaters have recommended over the years include soaking pads in a combination of vinegar and water, pet odor sprays, even vodka! Experiment and see what works best against your own potent perfume.

Or, you can try to reduce the amount of sweat your pads soak up in the first place. Ivanna S. Pankin of the San Diego Derby

Dolls recommends making pad condoms by cutting up old socks and t-shirt sleeves and sticking them between your skin and your protective gear.

PHOTO BY MARC "STALKERAZZI" CAMPOS

SMARTY PANTS OF TXRD LONESTAR ROLLERGIRLS CALLS OFF THE JAM AS SHE LANDS ON THE TRACK.

10. GET HURT.

Even if you are wearing all your protective gear, you are likely to get hurt doing derby. Here's our advice. Listen to your trainers and learn from them. There are ways you can skate and fall so as to minimize injuries. Even so, it's a rare rollergirl who skates for long without some sort of a scrape, scar, bruise, bump, contusion, or concussion.

You have a choice. You can fret about whether you might break your wrist or smash your collarbone. But we believe all that will do is increase the probability of that sort of thing occurring. That's because you'll be so worried about what *could* happen that you don't pay careful attention to what is *actually happening* around you.

Or you can recognize there is a potential for danger, and choose to focus instead on skating to the best of your abilities.

We've noticed that confident skaters usually fare better in the game and, on average, don't get hurt as much.

Some injuries are pretty obvious—if you break something or lose a tooth, you'll know it. If something like this happens at a practice or bout, there's a good chance your league-mates will take care of you and get you to the nearest emergency room. Many leagues have paramedics on call at bouts or will call an ambulance if one is required.

Some injuries leave marks, burns, or bruises. We wear these like badges of honor. Don't be surprised if you see derby girls pulling down their pants to compare huge purple welts, splotches of burned skin known as "track rash," or a nice swath of "fishnet burn"—the waffled telltale sign of a fall in fancy stockings.

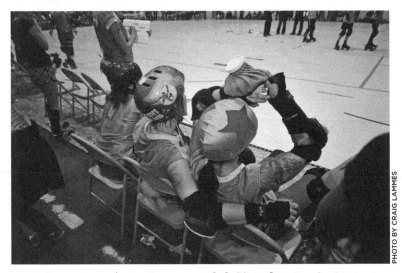

DEMI GORE OF THE ATLANTA ROLLERGIRLS SUPPORTS HER TEAM FROM THE SIDELINE AS SHE ICES AN INJURED HAND.

But many injuries are subtle and utterly invisible. You may over-extend yourself doing a crossover and pull your groin. It will smart, but you'll still be able to skate. Another skater might slam you so hard your ribs get bruised. But if you've got a high tolerance for pain, you might be inclined to keep skating for several more hours.

Once again, you have a choice here, and this is a really important one. Only you can judge if you are well enough to keep skating. Pushing through pain is something encouraged in derby—a good coach will want you to test the boundaries of what you think you can do. But, you can also do serious damage if you continue skating while injured.

What's more, if you're in a world of pain, there's a good chance you won't be able to focus as much on your form. If you're not paying attention, you're more likely to fall and you might wind up injuring someone else, too. So please, be thoughtful when you get hurt and remember that it's better to hold off on skating for a few hours, days, or weeks than it is to do something that would leave you or someone else unable to skate for months or years.

11. GET ON A TEAM.

Once you've learned how to skate you'll be itching to play in a bout. So you'll want to earn a spot on a team. Different leagues have different protocols regarding team placement.

Some will have you join a pool of sub-players first so you can learn more about how the game is played while helping fill open spots for skaters who go out of town or get injured. Many leagues will make you try out to become part of a sub-pool or team. These auditions usually include a mix of testing basic skating skills, like stopping, jumping and skating backward, as well as some scrimmaging to see what you can do in action.

Some leagues will let you request which team you would like to be placed on; others will not. Either way, earning a spot on a team is very exciting. You'll either be given or get to make your own uniform. You'll go to team-only practices to learn your team's secret language and strategies. Many teams also like to hang out together off-skates doing everything from wine-tastings to jumping out of airplanes. These are great ways to bond and to learn more about your fellow skaters.

12. SKATE YOUR FIRST BOUT!

If you stick with derby long enough, you'll get to one of the most exciting moments in your derby career—skating in your very first bout. As the date approaches you'll probably find yourself ridiculously excited and painfully nervous.

If possible, try to find ways to relax before your big debut. Ask other skaters what their pre-game rituals are and see what works for you. Some girls like to skate a little bit the night before; others like to stay off their wheels for at least a night or two so they can rest up. Some skaters like to eat a big carb-filled meal prior to a bout so they have plenty of energy. Others find if they try to eat, nerves will quickly have them running for the ladies' room. Hydrating before the big game is usually a good idea. But if you have a small bladder, be careful—nothing is worse than needing to pee when you're on the starting line.

There are two pieces of advice we feel are fairly safe to dole out to all first-time skaters. Plan your boutfit (what you'll wear during the game) in advance. Freaking out the day of your game because you're rushing all over town looking for just the right pair of magenta tights is the last thing you need!

And most importantly, *have fun*. Sure, at your first game you will want to impress your teammates, league-mates, and the friends and family who show up to watch. But don't get down on yourself if you mess up a few basic blocks or fail to score a single point. As much as you may have trained prior to your first game, there are some skills you can't get until you are there with the crowd watching. Don't beat yourself up too much—there are plenty of opposing blockers to do that job!

And remember, winning isn't everything. If you focus too much on whether your team is the victor, you probably won't enjoy it. Some of the best games we ever skated were ones we lost, but had a great time doing so.

WINDY CITY ROLLERS OF CHICAGO
BATTLE GOTHAM GIRLS OF NEW YORK

PHOTO BY KERRY MCCLAIN

Derby and Dating

FOR MANY, DERBY is the perfect venue to find best friends, partners in crime, and chummy adversaries. For others, it has also proven to be the stage for a deeper rendezvous—a bona fide Chuck Woolery-style love connection.

It would be inconceivable to imagine that a sport attracting self-confident men and women—

PHOTO BY MARC "STALKERAZZI" CAMPOS

straight, gay, bisexual, and those who experiment in the so-called "derby curious" realm—as anything other than a hotbed of romantic opportunity. But, like many rollergirls themselves, derby romances can go both ways. To keep your roller relationships healthy, we suggest you follow the Big Four Rules of Derby Dating:

1. Join Derby to Become a Hot Piece of Ass, Not to Get One.

Don't think for a minute that you can pop into a few practices, snag some tail, and get out with your reputation, your pride, and your safety intact. Creeps have short lifespans in the sport. Also, disrespecting a rollergirl's or derby dude's sport by reducing it to a glorified meat market is as dangerous as spitting on his or her mother.

2. Don't Forget the Derby Part of Your Derby Relationship.

Sure, you might be falling in love, but you're already in a relationship with your team. Don't let your googly eyes and mushy heart get in the way of your derby duties. Glitter HitHer of Jet City Rollergirls says of her relationship with league-mate Maiden Hades, "Talk about competitiveness before it becomes a wedge between you." If you have to hit your girl on the track, send her to the penalty box, or watch someone else give her the old suicide block, you'd better figure out how to do that . . . and fast. Don't put your relationship before your team during derby work hours, or resentment will rear its head.

3. Get To Know Each Other Off The Track.

The last thing you want to do is wake up one day and realize that derby is the only thing you have in common with your sweetie. Shoot to Kill, photographer for the Chicago Outfit, advises that you "get to know the real girl behind the derby girl before you go shackin' up." She and her girlfriend, Outfit skater Maul E. Hatchet, have a rule against talking derby before bed each night. Dispense with derby names when you leave the venue, and put aside some time for yourselves that doesn't involve putting wheels on your feet. Of course, sometimes that's easier said than done. "From February through November there are zero weekends that are free of some derby events," says Bazooka Joe of Pioneer Valley Roller Derby, whose girlfriend is league-mate Pink Panzer, "We have to make real efforts to say 'no' once in a while."

But eventually, one of the greatest benefits of being in a relationship with someone else in derby can be the sharing of love for the sport. Kitty Decapitate of the Victorian Roller Derby League in Melbourne,

Australia, says of her referee boyfriend, Flat Track Bully, "It's great to be able to share this thing which is my life with him . . . all the highs, lows, the gossip. He's, of course, my biggest critic (in a good way) and supporter." They were even once honored by *The Times* of London as "the Posh and Becks of roller derby."

4. Develop an Exit Strategy.

Only one relationship in your life will be your last, so do talk about what your plan will be if this is one of those that will come crashing down around you. Maul E. Hatchet advises, "If someone is about to date someone in derby, they have to accept the fact that it may not last forever, and you can't expect your ex to disappear from the derby world when you break up. It's gonna be awkward." In other words, there is no sole custody when it comes to derby divorces.

Dating within this community is like dating someone at the office, only worse. When you break up, you won't just have to see them a lot, they'll also be hitting you. Trust us, having your body assaulted by the one who broke your heart is a whole new level of suckage. Make the breakup plan, then mentally tuck it into your skate bag and hope you never have to use it.

At this point, dating in derby may seem more daunting than dreamy. But, your derby family will be there for you when your heart hurts and this sport can foster some incredible, long-lasting relationships, too. For example, Derby News Network co-founder Hurt Reynolds happened to be visiting skater Mercy Less, currently of Duke City Derby, the day her marriage fell apart. "He probably heard it explode," she remembers. A couple of years later, at the 2008 Nationals in Portland, Hurt proposed and the two are now happily married to each other.

9

If you can't Be an Athlete, Be an Athletic Supporter!

PHOTO BY KERRY MCCLAIN

UP UNTIL NOW, we've focused mostly on skaters—since they're the main focus of this sport. But roller derby wouldn't exist were it not for plenty of other people dedicating their time and talents. This sport is a bit like an iceberg. While the skaters are the impressive and photogenic beauties above

175

water, there's also a vast ocean of support without which we'd quickly drown.

We need coaches to teach us, refs to keep us in line, announcers to explain what the hell is going on . . . and, of course, where would we be were it not for the amazing fans who turn out to watch the bouts?

If you find the siren lure of derby calling to you, but fear you don't have the free time to be a competitive skater, or are worried about the possible physical risks, you may want to consider one of the following derby "careers."

ANNOUNCER

JOB DESCRIPTION: An announcer or commentator is a person behind the microphone at derby bouts who explains and entertains. Some announcers handle the play-by-play of a bout, some provide colorful commentary, and a skilled few manage to pull off both simultaneously.

A big part of this gig is informing and educating the audience, which is crucial given that roller derby isn't a sport most people grew up with, says Reverend Norb, announcer for the Fox Cityz Foxz in Appleton, Wisconsin. "You don't play it in gym class or in the backyard with the neighbor kids," he explains, "so people's minds will start wandering almost immediately at a bout. It's the announcer's job to continually rope their attention back in to the game."

But, derby announcers must be careful not to give too much away either. When you watch an NBA game on television, players can't hear the commentators. But derby bouts are live. Even at a venue with crappy acoustics, skaters may hear the play-by-play calls, and that could change the course of the game. That's why announcers aren't allowed to reveal the jammer's position as they head in to score.

There are also plenty of times during a bout when there's *no* skating happening—maybe there's a time-out or the refs need to take a few minutes to sort out a call. This is when commentators have to keep everyone entertained and engaged. It's their responsibility to keep the crowd amped, which can be tough during a blow-out game, when any passing shiny object poses a serious threat to the audience's attention.

Though not required, many commentators take on their own derby names and personas. A special boutfit can help distinguish an announcer and adds to the entertainment value. Some commentators like to develop trademark lines and other schtick. Mike Whitely and Tim Murphy, the original commentators for BGGW and then the TXRD Lonestar Rollergirls, have referred to the jammer moving through the pack "Like a hot knife through butter" so many times, you'd think Land O'Lakes had them on payroll.

THIS JOB MIGHT BE FOR YOU IF: Those who can't skate—commentate! The announcer gig is a great one for folks who love the sport, but aren't comfortable on wheels. Thorough understanding of rules is a must, as is the ability to talk for long stretches without a script. Knowing a little bit about a lot of stuff is a plus, notes Reverend Jim of the Burning River Roller Girls, "I can transition from *BJ and the Bear* references to Kegel exercises smoothly."

Like the good reverend, you, too, will need a healthy dose of confidence if you want to announce. A nice voice surely comes in handy, too. If you have a Rain-Man-like ability to remember skater names, numbers, the list of sponsors, and the address of the after-party that night—you were born to announce!

THIS JOB MIGHT NOT BE FOR YOU IF: Friends tell you your jokes remind them of their fifth grade math teacher. You cannot resist the temptation to yell when the lead jammer is approaching the pack. You have never in your life been able to successfully start the wave at a sporting event. You have the attention span of . . . ahem! Hello?? Hey *you*! We're talking here . . . ah, never mind.

WHY THIS GIG ROCKS: You have one of the best seats in the house. Do your job well and you may soon have some fans of your own.

PROFILE: Randy Pan the Goat Boy

PHOTO BY MICHAEL COYOTE

Announcers do it . . . and then tell everybody. Yuk, yuk, yuk. But seriously folks, it takes a good sense of humor and the gift of gab to be a roller derby announcer. Jake Merriman, a.k.a. Randy Pan the Goat Boy, has plenty of both. That's how he landed his gig as an announcer with the Rat City Rollergirls of Seattle.

Q: What do you think an announcer's job should entail?

RANDY PAN THE GOAT BOY: It should be about interpreting the sport of roller derby to an audience. Describing it is usually redundant (and what most announcers do). Entertainment is important, but still lands second to interpretation. It's not enough for an audience to know what's happening, but they also need to know why it's happening. If an announcer's doing her or his job right, then the audience knows what's going on just as much as we do.

Q: What do you wear when you announce?

RP: Cheesy leisure suit. Standard WFTDA announcer wear. I do have to rock sunglasses, a clam-shell necklace, chest hair, and a lot of hair gel . . . you know, to stand out.

Q: Do you have any trademark lines or schtick you are known for?

RP: I'm known for jumping around a lot. If there's track-side seating, I'll high-five the entire front row for intros. Oh yeah, I bleat like a goat, I guess that's my "line".

Q: What is the best part of being an announcer?

RP: For me it's being a part of a revolution. Not to be hokey, but that's what I truly feel roller derby is. It's the biggest "fuck you" to the status quo (sports status quo, male-dominated-anything status quo, corporate-Satans-running-everything status quo, etc.).

To be a guy involved in a revolution run by women is a special privilege. Granted, that puts me on the ass end of the totem pole, but I can hang there for a change, it's about time.

Tied for that is the life of it all. What I mean is, when you're doing derby you are truly engaged in living, not just waiting to die. You're taking an opportunity that life has given you, as opposed to watching other people do it. There's so much love that comes with this. You're in a community where everyone supports each other and loves each other for it, even if we all don't like each other. So yeah, best part is revolution, life, and love. Goddamnit, I sound like a hippy, I better go eat a fucking steak now.

Q: What advice would you give to a new announcer just getting started?

RP: Watch lots of bouts, know the rules, watch lots of bouts, know the hand signals, watch lots of bouts, learn the functions of an NSO, watch lots of bouts, listen to as many different announcers as you can, watch lots of bouts, have fun, watch lots of bouts, know your limit, watch lots of bouts.

Oh yeah, and don't be a douche bag. This is about the skaters, not you.

Q: What's the biggest mistake you've ever made as an announcer?

RP: Well, it turns out that saying an entire league's fan base is white supremacist doesn't go over very well. They hate that actually. It's funny, but they hate that.

WHY THIS GIG SUCKS: There's huge potential to get things wrong. You might say "That was a fantastic block by Viagra Falls," when it was in fact Ruby Bruiseday who made the hit.

Cincinnati Rollergirls announcer The Tank remembers misreading the name Deep Threat and introducing a skater as Deep Throat. "The usual applause," he says, "was replaced instead by awkward silence."

Reveal a team's strategy and you may find yourself attacked by an angry mob of skaters. If fans don't understand what's going on, they may well blame you.

INSIDER ADVICE: Carolina Rollergirls announcer Ryan Parker, a.k.a. Rockerboy, puts it well, "Know the rules. Know the skaters. Be brief." He recommends listening to NASCAR radio for inspiration. "They make you see with your ears."

Yes, you want to keep the crowd riled up, but it's uncouth to take sides and root for a team from the announcer's booth. Single Malt Scott learned that the hard way when announcing a double-header game for Montreal Roller Derby. He had the crowd boo the visiting league. Tempers escalated, the audience got rowdy, and when the home team lost both games, things got ugly. "As the last whistle blew, they started tossing the empty beer cans at the track," he recalls. "It was an aluminum rain. It was a sight to see, but a horrible mess."

HIGHLIGHTS IN HISTORY: The Dust Devil, the inaugural inter-league derby tournament held in 2006, was a real turning point for roller derby announcers. Up until then, many commentators flew solo at hometown bouts or worked with the same folks, folks they knew well, time and again.

All that changed at Dust Devil. A small group of announcers flew in from various corners of the country only to find themselves calling high-stakes bouts with people who they had literally just met. Mad Rollin' Dolls announcer Randy Hughes, a.k.a. Bob Noxious, remembers it well. "Everybody was nervous because you didn't know if you'd be good or bad or if people would showboat."

But that anxiety quickly melted. The small crew of commentators learned from one another and brainstormed on announcing techniques that have since become the derby industry standards. During one of the tourney bouts, things got rather heated and play-by-play announcer Jim "Koolaid" Jones of the Texas Rollergirls tried to keep the crowd calm. Sitting next to him, Tuscon announcer Jeff Mann commended Koolaid by dubbing him a "Voice of Reason."

"We ended up as a bro-rority," says Bob Noxious of the mostly male posse gathered at the Dust Devil. "We became the subculture of the subculture."

After they all returned home, Bob wanted to make sure his new buddies stayed connected, so he started an online group. Naturally, he called it the Voices of Reason.

"We're definitely the AV club geeks of roller derby," says Koolaid Jones of derby announcers. "While the rollergirls are skipping class to smoke in the girls room and get a bootleg tattoo under the bleachers, we're asking Mr. Kotter if we can run the projector. So it's pretty amazing to all of a sudden have this larger group of people who understood the unique position of being the lone nerd in a room of powerful, beautiful, and, most of all, cool women."

REFEREE

JOB DESCRIPTION: As in other sports, the referee's job is to make sure everyone abides by the rules. Since roller derby has a lot of rules, derby refs have a lot of duties.

These duties start well before a bout begins—refs make sure skaters aren't wearing jewelry that could hurt others in a pile-up, that they have their mouth guards, and they check to see if helmets are on and fitting snugly.

During a game, refs are tasked with counting points; communicating with the announcers, scorekeepers, and team captains; keeping track of jam clocks and game clocks; and stopping the action in case of injury. On top (or should we say underneath) all of this, there's a good chance a ref is wearing roller skates, too!

Clad in traditional black and white stripes, derby refs are also known as "zebras" and this species comes in many varieties. There are **jammer referees** who focus on the point-scoring skaters, making sure they don't cut the track and indicating who is lead jammer. **Pack referees** must mind multiple skaters at a time as they watch for penalties. Like the jammer refs, some pack refs do their job from the infield. Other pack refs observe from the periphery of the track where they get a unique vantage point on the action.

Minding this zeal of zebra is a **head referee**—the grand poobah of the striped brigade—who is ultimately responsible for all calls. The head ref also sorts out which duties are filled by the rest of the herd.

Refs blow the whistle indicating when each jam starts and finishes. They provide structure to a bout, making sure it has a defined beginning, middle, and end . . . an end in which one team wins. "I believe derby refs function as narrators of the game," explains Hambone, who signed on as a ref with the Gotham Girls shortly after his wife Ginger Snap joined the league. "Derby is a very unique sport in that the game play doesn't stop after fouls are committed or after points are scored. The referees, thus, play an important storytelling role."

Many refs also view their roles as guardians. Remember, rules exist in large part to keep skaters safe. "That's why we call penalties," explains Brother Grim, who refs in Australia, "It's not always because we're malicious bastards."

Like the skaters, referees often have to learn various sets of rules for bouts at home, away games, and tournaments. Refs also have to bone up on how to communicate penalties. Since bouts usually get loud, zebras indicate their calls—everything from "blocking with the head" to "insubordination"—through an elaborate system of hand signals.

NORTH STAR ROLLER GIRLS REF BUSTER HYMAN WATCHES SKATER MEDUSA AS SHE CALLS OFF THE JAM

THIS JOB MIGHT BE FOR YOU IF: You want to skate, but don't have enough free time to commit to being a playing skater. You used to skate, and you were injured and aren't able to compete anymore. Whistles and stopwatches turn you on and you enjoy the slimming effects of vertical stripes. Like a cop, you relish in having authority, providing safety, and enforcing rules.

THIS JOB MIGHT NOT BE FOR YOU IF: You are a big fan of a certain team or skaters and cannot restrain your love for them. Refs *must* be impartial.

You don't particularly enjoy people screaming that you're: blind, stupid, an asshole, or all of the above, and then some. You are even remotely afraid of rollergirls and their temper.

The song "Hand Jive" from *Grease* gives you the willies, mimes really creep you out, or you still believe that pointing is rude. Trust us, we've seen professional shadow puppeteers who use their hands less than derby refs!

WHY THIS JOB ROCKS: You really can't get much closer to the action than being a ref. And, you get to enjoy the sport the same way players do—rolling on skates. When you are a ref, you get the adrenaline rush of competition without having to suffer the blows of defeat. "The refs *always* win," remarks Gia De Los Muertos of the L.A. Enforcers. And unlike being a skater on a team, she adds, "We work *every* game. We skate *every* jam. "

Katja B. Autchez (say it aloud and it's the perfect name for a ref—"caught ya biotches!") likes the maternal aspect of the gig. As a referee with the Bellingham Roller Betties and the Dockyard Derby Dames of Tacoma, Katja says she busts skaters who break the rules in hopes that no one breaks a leg. "If my calls keep one skater from going to the hospital, then it is well worth it for me!"

WHY THIS JOB SUCKS: You can't please all of the people all of the time. This is something refs know all too well. Even if you make a good call, someone will probably disagree with what you saw. Make a mistake and you will most definitely hear about it from other refs, the crowd, and the skaters.

Sometimes, it takes a thick skin to deal with the backlash. "Everyone makes mistakes," says James Alonso, the Midwestern ref otherwise known as 19. "If you are straight-up about them quickly, they can be fixed, if not, then you are costing someone a fair shot at winning the game."

Many refs report they have nightmares about bad calls years after they happen.

INSIDER ADVICE: Know the rules! It's not uncommon to hear refs at a bar sounding like crazed mathematicians . . . gleefully citing WFTDA Rules 4.0 Section 9.2.11.6. (Head ref's decision on a call is final). If you want to keep up, Katja B. Autchez recommends stashing copies of your league's rule set everywhere: next to your bed, in the bathroom, and at work, so you can get to know them like the back of your wrist guard covered hand.

Keep a cool head, and remember, just like the skaters they watch over, referees need to work together as a team. Ref Hambone cites his years playing cello in orchestras and chamber groups as some of the best preparation for his current gig. "Those are situations where you have very similar elements: a general script to work from, lots of teammates, hours and hours of practice together, a physical challenge, the need to improvise, plus an audience to communicate with," he explains. And if you do hit a sour note, he advises, it's not the end of the world. Like a musician, hopefully with lots of practice, you'll make less of them.

HIGHLIGHTS IN HISTORY: At RollerCon 2009, the observers became the observed! On a sweltering Friday afternoon, two co-ed teams comprised of refs and skaters scrimmaged on Fremont Street in front of hundreds of people. It was the Co-Ed Cripplers versus the Grammercy Refs.

Co-Ed Crippler Team Captain Sephra Oare is a ref with the Emerald City Roller Girls. She says the transition from watching the skaters play to playing herself was exhilarating . . . and a bit confusing. "I will admit, I was a bit of the deer in the headlights as far as entering and exiting the penalty box," she recalls.

A Co-Ed Crippler named Speed Bump, of the Treasure Valley Rollergirls (Boise, Idaho), said switching roles gave him a whole new appreciation of what it takes to abide by the rules. "Being the head ref for my league, I still got two majors in thirty minutes," he says. But it showed him something. "You may know the rules inside and out, but it's a bitch when you are on the track."

PROFiLE: Justice Feelgood Marshall

PHOTO BY ADAM TOLMAN

If roller derby had a Supreme Court, Justice Feelgood Marshall would most certainly deserve a spot on it. He wears many hats, or should we say helmets, in derby, as a referee for Baltimore's Charm City Roller Girls, a member of the men's Harm City Homicide team, and a staff writer for the Derby News Network.

Q: So, Justice, how did you get into derby?

JUSTICE FEELGOOD MARSHALL: A college friend of mine from Baltimore had moved to New York City and happened to be one of the original Gotham Girls, Lil' Red Terror. It just so happened that I was driving cross-country to Baltimore the week before their first-ever bout in November 2004, so I took a route that took me through New York just in time to see it. I had an absolutely incredible time, and I remember going back to Baltimore thinking it was a shame that nothing that cool would ever get started in a mid-

DOWN AND DERBY

size city like Baltimore. Lo and behold, six months later, my girlfriend's roommate sees a flyer for a start-up league called the Charm City Roller Girls and gets us to come with her to an open skate. Best decision I made in my whole life.

Q: How'd you pick your derby name?

JFM: Since I was going to be a ref, I wanted something that had to do with the law, and since I'm black, and that's somewhat out of the ordinary in this sport, I wanted something that was going to address it head-on. I was kicking around a few names of that nature, but when I remembered that Thurgood Marshall had grown up in Baltimore, it was pretty much locked in.

Q: What do enjoy most about your job as ref?

JFM: As a head ref, I really enjoy the challenge of being right at the center of barely controlled chaos on the track, and people losing their minds in the stands. Everybody else in the building is running at incredibly high levels of adrenaline during a bout, and it's a unique experience to be tasked with being the one person who absolutely must remain calm and keep the game running smoothly. For such a simple game, there can be some extremely convoluted rule scenarios that unexpectedly crop up for the first time ever during a bout, and it's challenging, but fun, to solve them quickly and fairly under so much pressure.

Q: What are some common misperceptions about refs?

JFM: Mostly that we're in it as a power trip. Fans—and really, a lot of players—don't realize that refs actually have amazingly little power to do anything discretionary. The rules have consistently been getting more and more objective, which has its benefits and drawbacks, but it means refs rarely have a choice about making calls. Either you committed an illegal action or you didn't.

Q: What do you see as the future of roller derby?

JFM: Not everybody agrees with me, but I personally hope to see more integration between men's and women's events—more high-profile men's/women's doubleheaders, more co-ed expo bouts, that kind of thing. I, for one, wouldn't be playing this sport if it weren't for the women who introduced me to it in the first place, and I like sharing the experience with them. Nothing would make me happier than eventually seeing a crazy week-long national championship tournament with women's, men's, and co-ed winners for both flat and banked track. I think it'll happen someday, but probably not soon. I just hope to still be skating when it does!

Q: You've lived up to your law-abiding name both on and off the track. Care to share the story of what happened at Dougherty's Pub?

JFM: Hah—a bunch of Homicide skaters went to a local bar after practice one night when it was almost totally empty—just us, the bartender, and one waitress, who happened to be the girlfriend of a Homicide player at the time. About an hour after we start drinking, the waitress runs out of the kitchen and says there's a guy trying to break in through the basement. We all run back there and the bartender is barely able to hold the door closed as some guy is kicking and shouldering it from the other side. We were able to get to the door in time and put our weight on it to give him time to call 911 before the guy could break through.

It was kind of nerve-wracking, just because we never got a look at the guy and didn't know if he was armed or if it was more than just one person. But the cops came and arrested the dude, and it was a little funny because some of us were still wearing our practice uniforms, which are police-themed, and it was like the men's derby team of fake cops was quicker and more effective than the actual city policemen.

Plus we got free drinks for the rest of the night, which was pretty damn sweet.

NSO

JOB DESCRIPTION: No, this gig doesn't mean being a member of the National Symphony Orchestra or the Nurses Service Organization. In the world of derby, the NSO's are Non-Skating Officials. Like the refs, these folks help run the game and serve various administrative tasks, but they do so off-skates.

Some NSO's are **scorekeepers** who keep track of the total number of points, as communicated by the jammer refs. The **scoreboard operator** takes those numbers and shares them with the audience by posting it on either an old-school or digital scoreboard.

Penalty timers oversee the penalty box, or sin bin. They make sure an offending skater serves her time and that her team hits the track with the right number of players, given the penalty. **Penalty trackers** tally the number of penalties as doled out by the refs. They're the ones responsible for noticing when a skater has racked up so many penalties that it's time for her ejection.

THIS JOB MIGHT BE FOR YOU IF: You want to see this sport grow and thrive but you have no desire to do so on skates. You are good with numbers and stopwatches. You like efficiency and record keeping. You think the only thing cooler than derby is math.

While refs pride themselves on skills of observation, the NSO's are all about accuracy and attention to detail. "I don't make mistakes," declares Rita Her Rights of the Rat City Rollergirls, "I'm a Lightning Fist of Science!" That's a term used by all of Rat City's NSO's— they even wear white lab coats while tending to NSO duties.

THIS JOB MIGHT NOT BE FOR YOU IF: You are dyslexic. You enjoy getting drunk at bouts. You are easily distracted. Like the Teen Talk Barbie Doll, you've been known to say, "Math class is tough!"

WHY THIS JOB ROCKS: For those dealing with penalties, you may be keeping track of them, but you're not making the calls. This means you are usually safe from the wrath of irate skaters insisting on they're innocent.

IF YOU CAN'T BE AN ATHLETE, BE AN ATHLETIC SUPPORTER!

189

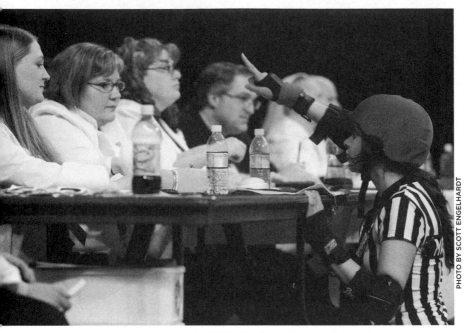

PHOTO BY SCOTT ENGELHARDT

FAT CITY'S LIGHTNING FISTS OF SCIENCE

Stats folks get to see very tangible proof of how skaters evolve and improve over time. Mathemagician is a stats guy for the Dutchland Derby Rollers of Lancaster, Pennyslvania. He says he loves seeing new skaters gain confidence as they reduce their penalties and improve their point scores. "I choose to support derby because it attracts empowered and self-assured individuals, who make very good friends," he said.

WHY THIS JOB SUCKS: If you think you're going to get to watch every second of each bout—think again. You have to spend a good deal of time during each game watching clocks and entering data. As Matt DeCaptitator, a statistician for several East Coast leagues attests, you need tremendous focus. "You must realize that you are there to do a job and not to watch the game," he explains. "If you are watching the bout, you are not doing stats, and if you are doing stats, you are not watching the bout."

INSIDER ADVICE: Head Stats guy c4 of the Mad Rollin Dolls in Wisconsin recommends spending as much time as possible before a bout checking out the skaters. "No, I'm not entirely a perv," he adds, "when you have a better idea of the numbers/names and what skaters look like, it's one less thing you have to think about while the wheels are rolling."

"Start slowly," recommends BiRoller Disorder with the Dutchland Derby Rollers. He suggests working your way up in the world of NSO's beginning with lineups; then moving to jam timing; and on to scoring and ultimately penalties.

Finally, Rita Her Rights reminds all NSO's that, like a good ref, they must be impartial. "Work to be as efficient as possible, so that your actions have as little impact on the game as possible," she says. "If we're doing our jobs right, then we should be invisible to the fans and the skaters."

HIGHLIGHTS IN HISTORY: L.A. Derby Dolls stats guy Mike Legat is better known throughout the country as Mike Snakeyes—a surname he picked up after he started dating skater Suzy Snakeyes. At a bout in the summer of 2009, Mike used his connections with the league's AV team and the announcers to plan a little something special right before half-time.

PHOTO BY MARC "STALKERAZZI" CAMPOS

MIKE "SNAKEYES" LEGAT PROPOSING TO ROBIN "SUZY SNAKEYES" RODENZWEIG AT A DERBY DOLLS BOUT.

The announcers asked the skaters to stay in the infield as a video featuring pictures of the couple set to the tune of a-ha's "Take on Me" played on the big scoreboard screens. Then, a number of Derby Dolls in the bleachers held up individual letter signs that spelled "*Suzy Snakeyes, Will You Marry Me?*" By that point, Mike was on bended knee on the banked track.

"She was completely surprised and overwhelmed," Mike recalls fondly, "Oh, and she said 'yes.'" That night Suzy left the track both a victor and a fiancé. "The rest of the night was a blur of love and support from friends, teammates, and people in the stands we'd never met," says the betrothed statistician. "It was truly an amazing way to start the next stage of my life with a roller derby girl."

COACH

JOB DESCRIPTION: A coach or trainer teaches rollergirls how to skate and play derby. Instructing fresh meat can mean starting with the absolute basics of how to put an elbow pad on correctly and how to stand up with wheels on your feet. Coaches may be the ones teaching skaters the rules of the sport once they've nailed down the rudimentary skills. They can share finer points about strategies and work individually with skaters to help them overcome obstacles.

Some derby trainers work with a league as a whole, some coaches focus on just one team, and others will do a bit of both. A league often nominates skaters from within its ranks to serve as trainers. Other coaches come from outside of a league.

To excel as a coach, you need a great set of eyes. One gal might not be able to do a basic move known as a T-stop because her hip is turned out too much; another might not be able to cross over because her knees aren't bent enough. It's a coach's job to assess and offer corrections that will help each individual progress.

Coach Pauly, one of derby's best known trainers, points out that you need to be an excellent communicator, with an ability to read people. "There are a ton of great skaters out there who are awesome technical skaters, but they don't know how to unlock the minds of the people they are trying to train." Sometimes a trainer needs to push skaters and make them work hard. Other times, they might need some tender encouragement. You might be called upon to be both a tough drill sergeant and a shoulder to cry on in the course of one night.

During bouts, some coaches are right there in the infield, offering advice and support with each jam. Other coaches like to observe the bout from the bleachers and watch the fruition of their hard work, beer in hand.

THIS JOB MIGHT BE FOR YOU IF: You know a lot about roller derby or skating in general and you adore teaching. You have boundless patience and don't feel the need to be the one in the limelight come game day. You are creative and can come up with lots of drills and exercises that improve understanding of the game. You are frequently asked to use your "inside voice" when talking at what you think is a quiet level. You are a bit of a sadist, but you also have an understanding of the "safe word" concept when your charges have had enough.

THIS JOB MIGHT NOT BE FOR YOU IF: You are a phenomenal skater, but find it difficult articulating how you do what you do. You don't consider yourself particularly adept at picking up on what makes a person tick. Hearing gals complain is like the sound of finger-nails on chalkboard to your ears.

You are looking to hook up with a rollergirl—there is a special ring of hell reserved for coaches looking to get laid.

WHY THIS JOB ROCKS: Watching skaters improve and grow can be incredibly rewarding. As Coach Pauly puts it, "For me, the best part about being a coach is watching a skater go from not knowing how to skate to playing on a top-seeded travel team. Knowing you had a part to play in it makes everything worthwhile."

Unlike a ref or NSO, you can unabashedly revel in the glory

193

when your team wins. Hooah!Girl, a trainer with the D.C. Rollergirls, was about to retire from derby when her team, the D.C. DemonCats, begged her to stay on and help them defeat the reigning champs. "They did everything I asked of them and more," Hooah!Girl recalls proudly. "Holding that trophy high over my head after our champ bout was one of the greatest senses of accomplishment I've ever experienced."

If you become known in the world of derby as a great trainer, you'll likely be invited to lend your services to other leagues. Coach Pauly has traveled everywhere from Edmonton, Canada to the wine country of California to train skaters. Trainer Smarty Pants, who also skates as a Holy Roller in Austin, has been flown from Texas to New Zealand and Australia to help fledgling leagues down under.

WHY THIS JOB SUCKS: Lest you forget, you are dealing with rollergirls, women known for powerful personalities and rebellious natures that may not mix well with authority figures. "The biggest challenge is dealing with all the different personalities, the different egos, and the general trouble that can occur when you get a group of strong, independent women together," says Ang Xiety, who coaches the Pile O Bones Derby Club in Saskatchewan, Canada.

INSIDER ADVICE: "All athletes are different," reminds New Zealand native Pieces of Hate, who knows this well as a professional skateboarder. Now a trainer and skater herself, Hate notes that some skaters like having orders barked at them while others need lots of encouragement and nurturing. "Find somewhere in the middle," she suggests, "and see what works best."

And here's a thought from the two of us, who also serve as trainers for the L.A. Derby Dolls: no one trainer can do it all for all skaters. Every coach has his or her own style and way of explaining things. What works well for one skater might not for another . . . so don't despair! If one of your skaters is struggling with something and you find yourself struggling to help her, don't feel ashamed about encouraging her to look to another coach for advice.

HIGHLIGHTS IN HISTORY: The typical derby practice lasts a few hours at most, and even the best coaches can only fit in so much into one practice. But imagine how much you could teach if you did nothing but derby all day and night! That's exactly what happens each year at the Blood & Thunder Training Camp.

PHOTO BY MICHAEL COYOTE

Black Dahlia, co-owner and editor of *Blood & Thunder Magazine*, dreamt this camp up based on her experiences going to a full-immersion gymnastics camp as a kid. "Everyone stayed in cabins, ate together, and spent downtime together," she remembers. "It was one of the best experiences of my life, and I saw a need in derby for something similar—a place where both skaters and coaches could come together to learn."

Held in places like San Diego, California, and New Plymouth, New Zealand, these four-day intensive camps bring together some of the best coaches in modern derby. Classes are focused on specific skills, such as starting with toe-stops, flipping the rail, and interpreting derby stats. There have even been sessions on sports hypnosis!

IF YOU CAN'T BE AN ATHLETE, BE AN ATHLETIC SUPPORTER!

DERBY TATTOOS

Roxy Rockett's self portrait tattoo
Arm tattoo of skater with braids

CONTRARY TO POPULAR BELIEF, having a tattoo is not a prerequisite to becoming a rollergirl. But, some stereotypes exist for a reason . . . that is to say a *lot* of us do have ink. And many derby girls sport tattoos with a skate-related theme.

J1 "Jabs" Abrams of the Chicago Outfit got a tattoo of her Riedell Vandal skates done on the back of her neck. Fellow rollergirl Cyanide Cupcake of the London Rollergirls did the work during a trip Jabs made to England. "I went with almost no money, stayed with someone I really didn't know, was injured from derby, and met some of the most awesome derby girls in the world," she recalls. "I wanted something for the rest of my life to remind me of where I was in my life at that point, and how good people can be."

For some girls, derby tattoos are a testament to all the effort they've poured into the sport. "I wanted it to remind myself of the hard work I put into derby and how proud my kids are of me," says Tenacious D. Lilah, who chose a sugar skull with axles and wheels instead of cross bones. This Treasure Valley Rollergirl says the tattoo symbolizes the "sweetness" of derby life. "Even the most bitter and bruised moments in derby hold fond memories and significance," she says.

Brat O'Tat's tattoo of the Red Stick Roller Derby logo
Leg tattoos of the skater holding up the stick

Tattoos can also be a way to celebrate one's dedication

to a derby team or league . . . especially when that tattoo is done on the inside of your bottom lip. That's where Kristy Norris, a.k.a. Violet Reaction, got hers done. The letters of R-S-R-D for Red Stick Roller Derby became a permanent part of her anatomy during a road trip to Austin. "It just felt right," Violet says of the experience. "It was a fun way to bond with a couple of my closest friends and teammates."

Many girls get tattoos of their skates or of their league logo, or in the case of Carolina Rollergirl Roxy Rockett, a three-quarters-sleeve full-color portrait of herself in derby action! We especially like Jenna Von Fury's tattoo. It's of her derby wife and fellow Garden State Rollergirl, Betty Brawl. Jenna wanted to pay tribute to her best friend and favorite skating partner, "She deserved a tattoo after blocking for me while jamming for the last two years!"

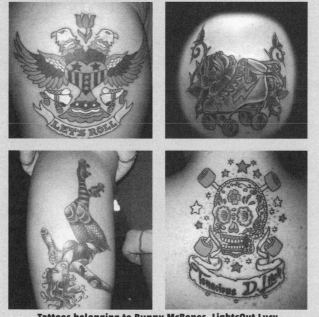

Tattoos belonging to Bunny McBones, LightsOut Lucy, Lethal Lavender, and Tenacious D. Lilah

Bunny: Eagles with "Let's roll"; Lightsout Lucy: Skate with lightning bolt; Lethal Lavender: Pinup roller girl on her back; and Tenacious D. Lilah: Sugar skull.

FAN

JOB DESCRIPTION: This job doesn't require a whole lot of work beyond buying a ticket and showing up to a game. But don't let that fool you into thinking this isn't an important role!

Sure, we could play derby without an audience, but that wouldn't be nearly as much fun! It also would make the sport nearly impossible to financially sustain. Derby supporters buy the tickets that allow us to rent venues and stay in business. Fans also inspire us to skate well and hit hard. A few good hoots and hollers can definitely amp a gal up, and nothing beats the rush of hearing your skate name chanted by the audience.

TXPD LONESTAR ROLLERGIRLS FAN

PHOTO BY PENNY SMITH

Don Lewis of Austin, Texas, recalls watching his first bout shortly before he turned sixty years old—"confusing as hell, but I loved it!" As a guy who races stock cars, Don found an affinity for derby, "I can identify with fighting one's way through hostile traffic in the turns!" He's been a regular fan ever since and even became a TXRD team sponsor.

Most derby supporters get into the sport by going to a bout in their hometown. But once they catch the bug, many fans travel to see games and tournaments in far-flung locales and meet up with fellow derby fanatics. Diehard fans from around the world will offer reports online so that other fans can keep up with the action remotely.

If you are a fan with a penchant for dressing up, you may want to consider being a mascot. Bob Burns, a product service associate for Lowe's in Edmond, Oklahoma, found his calling in the shape of a coyote costume. As OkiDoki Coyote he cheers on the Tornado Alley Rollergirls, and, really, what could be better than some roller derby action mixed with a life-size furry beast of prey doing the Hustle?

THIS JOB MIGHT BE FOR YOU IF: You love roller derby. You believe bouts are better if you have the freedom to drink during them. You have strong opinions and you like to share them, preferably at the top of your lungs. You have several free drawers ready to be filled with derby t-shirts.

THIS JOB MIGHT NOT BE FOR YOU IF: You have a solid belief that all "real" sports must include the use of a ball. To enjoy something, you need to feel like you are a part of its creation. You think all women should be demure and "ladylike," and aren't afraid to express this opinion in public.

WHY THIS JOB ROCKS: You get to watch derby—the best sport ever. And, unlike many other sports, there's a good chance you'll get to hang out with your favorite players before, during, and after a bout, and they'll be genuinely excited to see you. This personal

touch makes rooting for your favorite team especially thrilling.

You don't have to worry about being non-biased. Uber-fan Costa Ladeas, who's traveled throughout the country to watch bouts, says he'd never dream of filling another role in derby besides fan. "Once you join a league, you have to tow the party line, you lose your objectivity."

WHY THIS JOB SUCKS: Though derby tickets are often cheaper than tickets to other pro-sporting events, they're seldom free. Add up tickets, the merch you'll likely want to buy once you're at a bout, and travel costs, and you may soon notice that watching derby isn't necessarily a cheap hobby.

And don't think just because you're not working at bouts that your role won't require a significant chunk of your time. Phil Arnold, an economist also known as Derby Phil, goes to games about five times a month. He says it's tough finding enough time in the week to "watch derby, write recaps, make after-parties, work, and sleep."

INSIDER ADVICE: Don't be a letch. Seriously. Yes, we frequently wear low cut shirts and short skirts, but that is not an open invitation for you to get creepy on us.

If you think we beat up on each other, just wait and see the unique forms of abuse rollergirls will heap on any fan that gets out of line.

HIGHLIGHTS IN HISTORY: The Nashville Roller Girls are fortunate to have what may well be the coolest derby fan ever—Reilly Gabel. Reilly went to her first bout with her dad when she was ten. The excitement of getting an autograph from skater Hildabeast made her yell "OMG!" And thus, a fan known as OMG Rollergirl was born.

OMG Rollergirl is so smitten with derby that after bouts, she makes online videos of her recaps and shares them with the world via YouTube. OMG Rollergirl Report 5 opens with her bouncing up and down in her striped Hello Kitty shirt and doing air guitar

OMG ROLLERGIRL WITH LADY FURY OF THE NASHVILLE ROLLERGIRLS

to Ozzy's "Crazy Train." She goes on to single out a ref whose calls she didn't like. "He missed a false start . . . ." OMG Rollergirl cries, "I'm ten and I know a false start when I see it!"

Play your cards right, and this amazing fan may give you a special "OMG Hollah!" in one of her videos.

SALUTE THE OFFICERS IN THE DERBY ARMY!

One of the universally wonderful things about taking on any of the jobs mentioned above is that you're bound to make some great new buddies in your local league. But don't stop there! Learn from your brethren. Get in touch with your derby ilk online. Trust us, if it's something to do with derby, there's a special Internet group out there waiting for you. Go to other games and see how others do their jobs. We guarantee you'll get something out of it and make some amazing friends along the way.

IF YOU CAN'T BE AN ATHLETE, BE AN ATHLETIC SUPPORTER!

And, if you're feeling like none of these roles quite fit, but you still want to be involved in derby, don't worry. There's probably a spot on your local league just waiting for you. If you have a background in health, maybe you can be the league's next EMT or chiropractor. Have an amazing collection of music? See if you can DJ a bout. Are you exceptionally talented with tools? Volunteer to help your league build a banked track or lay down some sport court—you will earn big points with skaters.

Even if you don't think you have any special talents, if you have some free time and are willing to spend it on derby, we'll bet tickets to the next bout that your local league will find a way to put you to good use.

That's what Natalie Klein of Rochester, New York, did. Klein is a grad student working on her dissertation in psycholinguistics. But as Muffy Stopheles, she heads up the production crew, a.k.a. Team B*tch, for the Roc City Rollers.

She loves the feeling of accomplishment when they sell out a bout. And, like the skaters at the center of the sport, she gets a taste of what it's like to have an alter-ego in the derby world. "I love it," Muffy says, "when someone from my university department shows up at a bout and sees what I do when I'm not busy crunching data."

Dolly Rocket's Do's and Don'ts for Switching Leagues

SOMEWHERE ALONG THE WAY in your skating career, you may wind up moving to a new town for work, for school, for love, or just for the heck of it. Derby is derby, but no two leagues are exactly alike. When you enlist with a new group of girls, you may find yourself facing some changes.

Just take it from Dolly Rocket who's been a member of three different leagues. She started her career with Providence Roller Derby. She also spent a fair amount of time with the Boston Derby Dames while living in Rhode Island. Then, in 2007, she moved to Baltimore to be with her girlfriend, Joy Collision, and she joined the Charm City Rollergirls. She was kind enough to share her thoughts on making the transition to a new league.

As you can see, I have some experience switching leagues. I like to play roller derby, though apparently I can't sit still. While switching leagues for me was a really emotional experience, it wound up being great because now I feel like I have a home in two cities: Providence and Baltimore. Here are a few Do's and Don'ts to help you through the process.

DO take the time you need before trying out.

Life should come before roller derby. Moving to a new city can be really difficult on many levels—you don't know anyone, you don't know where anything is, you may not have a job or apartment, everything is up in the air for a while. Make sure you take the time to settle into your new life before adding yet another crazy change onto your plate. Don't join your potential new league until you are fully ready to commit to being a part of it. You don't want to be immediately labeled a flake! Understanding your own limits is very respectable and mature. If your new league is eager to grab you up, give them a loose time line as to when you will be ready to join, and try to be respectful of their tryout dates and transfer policies.

DON'T be a douche.

Though not a rule that I consistently follow, always a good general mantra. Yes, you have opinions about things, and you may very well be right, but you have to learn to work within the structure of your new league. Their administration, coaching, and skating styles, home team themes, *whatever,* may bug the hell out of you, but don't come into your new league like a whirlwind complaining and trying to change everything. Before you get all crazy and control freaky, you need to establish trust and friendship with your new league-mates. Try to see the good things about your switch and be open to new ways of doing things. You never know, it may actually be better than your old league. When the time is right, have positive and constructive criticisms about problems you see. Please make sure you bring any criticisms or suggestions to the appropriate people. Offer to help with any changes you feel would benefit your new league.

If you're Dolly Rocket: You'll be a big-mouthed douche. I showed up in CCRG at a time of transformation for the league. I wound up being a big catalyst for a lot of policies and procedures to be written. Coming from a more experienced league at the time, I think people were looking to me for a lot of answers, or just generally looking to me to be "that guy" that was going to shake things up. A lot of CCRGers wound up quitting because of CCRG's transition to a more competitive league, but it helped to make CCRG what it is today.

DO let go of your old league. Just a little bit.

It can be really hard to say good-bye to your friends and league-mates, however a certain professional divide has to happen once you are no longer a member of your old league. Once you move, you don't have to continue to do tons of administrative work for them. Yes, that would be very, very nice of you. But you need to also make time to do some work for your new league, learn about your new city, settle into your new job/apartment/school, and make new friends. Have a nice good-bye party for yourself, and be clear about when you are going to stop your duties. Make sure you train someone new into your old positions and give them all of the information they will need before you leave.

DON'T completely drop your old league all together.

They are your friends! Visit practices every once in a while, and make sure you make time for them at national derby events, it's always a nice blast from the past. If they ask you for advice, give it, and don't be shy to ask them for help, too.

Also, don't be totally weird should the day ever come that you have to play against them. Talk to your old and new league about how you feel about it, set some boundaries that everyone can respect. Things like, "Hey coach, I reserve the right to take myself out of a line up if this gets too emotional;" or "I can't jam against my derby wife;" or " I really want to jam against my derby wife!"

If you tell everyone what you need in advance, you won't wind up being an embarrassing emotional mess, hopefully. Remember, we play derby for fun, and if it ain't fun, you gotta find a way to make it that way.

DO be yourself.

Meeting a new group of girls can be intimidating. Make sure you show them your true colors, don't pretend to be someone you're not. Keeping that up can be really exhausting. Let your new league know what your strengths and weaknesses are as a skater and as a person. People always appreciate honesty.

If you're Dolly Rocket: You'll do this and be surprised that people like you anyway. Well, some people.

10

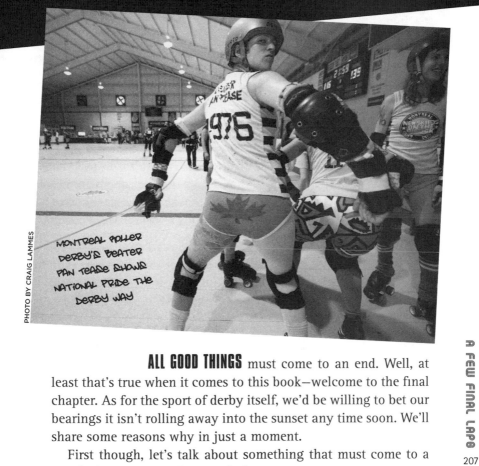

MONTREAL ROLLER DERBY'S BEATER PAN TEASE SHOWS NATIONAL PRIDE THE DERBY WAY

A FEW FINAL LAPS

ALL GOOD THINGS must come to an end. Well, at least that's true when it comes to this book—welcome to the final chapter. As for the sport of derby itself, we'd be willing to bet our bearings it isn't rolling away into the sunset any time soon. We'll share some reasons why in just a moment.

First though, let's talk about something that must come to a conclusion sooner or later: a derby career.

YOU'VE GOT TO KNOW WHEN TO HOLD 'EM...
KNOW WHEN TO FOLD 'EM

We idolize Ann Calvello for many reasons: she had a feisty exterior, a heart of gold, and an unsurpassed dedication to derby. But beyond all that, the woman had amazing stamina. She skated more than half a century. Ann played this brutal sport way longer than either of us has been alive on this planet!

There are days when we wish we could do the same. It would be incredible to proudly claim that we skated derby for six freakin' decades and lived to tell. But there are other things we love, too—watching *So You Think You Can Dance* on weeknights instead of trudging off to practice; having feet that don't provoke a gasp of disgust from the poor lady giving us pedicures; not being bothered by the latest league drama; spending derby-free quality time with loved ones.

After several wonderful years of skating competitively, we both made a decision, a really difficult decision, to retire. How do you know when it's your time? That's a tough one. Chances are, you will always wonder how much better you might have become as a skater if you had stuck with it. You'll realize that when you resign, you'll eventually miss out on all sorts of derby experiences. You'll be left with the problem of figuring out what the hell you are going to do next to stay in shape.

You may also find yourself a feeling adrift without the derby identity that's become an integral part of who you are. "I've been Kammi Kazi for almost six years," remarks L.A. Derby Doll Alissa Stahl, aka Kammi, who confessed having serious qualms about retiring. "Roller derby made me a better person and taught me to believe in myself. It introduced me to a world of bright and beautiful women who also believed in me. I was afraid of losing that connectedness."

Scary indeed. Which is why we recommend talking with your derby friends, teammates, and some of your non-derby pals before you decide to retire. But ultimately, you should go with your gut—you'll know when it's time. For Kammi, who eventually did retire in the summer of 2009, it was her sense of responsibility that sealed the deal. "I figured I should retire with grace and dignity," she says, "before I became that teammate who is never around, and when she does show up she's a total crab."

If you can help it, don't pull a Sarah Palin and split before your league's season is finished. Your team will probably prefer it if you stick around until their final game—but sometimes that's not possible. You may get a new job in a different city. Or, health reasons might require you to stop. And we can't tell you how many derby careers have been cut short when players discover they're pregnant.

No matter why or when you retire, chances are the pains you once felt from post-practice bruises will be replaced by pangs of remorse. As one former skater puts it, "Giving up roller derby is tougher than giving up heroin." We concur—derby can easily become an addiction.

And, like breaking an addiction, you have a couple of choices when it comes to hanging up your skates. You can go for the "Band-Aid approach"—rip derby out of your life quickly and don't look back. This is easy enough to do if you split town and head to a derby-free destination.

But if you're not one to let go of things easily, we advise weaning yourself off the sport slowly. As you know, there are many ways to stay involved with your league without actively competing. There's a good chance your league could benefit from your knowledge and experience if you start coaching, reffing, announcing, or volunteering your services in some other way.

PROFILE: Ms. D'Fiant

Sometimes, though we hate to admit it, life has to come before derby. Sometimes, that life is a brand new one—such as little Tucker, the potential future roller boy who recently gestated in the prime blocking zone of Heather Hamilton, a.k.a. Ms. D'Fiant. Pregnancy has marked the end of the derby road for many a skater, but for this Angel City Derby Girls stalwart, it was merely a happy pause in a long career.

Q: How involved are you in roller derby?

MS. D'FIANT: I skate for Angel City Derby Girls, and I am a team manager and Gaming Commissioner for the league. I'm also WFTDA rep and the WFTDA Stats and Rankings Chair.

Q: What tactics do you find successful in balancing full-time derby and a full-time relationship with your husband, Ben?

MD: I am awful at balancing full-time derby with anything else. As a result, Ben (a.k.a. Captain of the Swim team, AC/DG announcer) made a rule that I sometimes follow—one derby event a weekend. This includes: bouts, birthdays, fundraisers, etc. Does not include: tournaments, away games, or practices. This may sound extreme, but those of you who are in the know understand that you can fill your weekend, week, year, or life with derby events.

Q: We know you both had discussed a desire to have children in the near future. What was your original strategy to figure out the best timing for this?

MD: Part of my Gaming Commissioner job is planning the season schedule for my league. This is a great job for me, because I'm an obsessive planner. So naturally, when it came to planning a family I chose to do it around my derby schedule. We knew the team looked good for Regionals 2009 back in 2008, so I penciled in a baby for 2010.

Q: And how'd that work out for you?

MD: Apparently I can't plan everything. We were pregnant in May 2009 and I only have derby to blame. I had a particularly rough month training for/shooting our derby workout video, pulling off the tournament we hosted, the WFTDA annual meeting, then a game against Sin City. Totallllllly missed my yearly appointment with my doc, and got knocked up right before Vegas. Consequently, my then-unborn child survived his first game and one night in Vegas. He is gonna be a bruiser!

Q: Who knew about your pregnancy first—your team or your family?

MD: My team. After three seasons of play, people look at you a little suspiciously if you suddenly don't feel like scrimmaging.

Q: What finally inspired you to let all of your family know?

MD: Well, we were waiting to tell our parents in person, which wasn't possible (due to distance) until after the first trimester. Our families are loud mouths, so we didn't tell a soul. That is until one night at Ben's cousin's house when they asked about my team's upcoming game. They all wanted to come and see the game since they had never seen me play before. I let them know that the game is still on but I'm not playing. The table fell awkwardly silent. One cousin fumbled over his words, but basically implied that I had been benched.

"What? Wait! Noooooo! I wasn't benched! Not this girl—travel team three seasons running, "Best Blocker 2008", prized pivot—my team loves me!"

(silence and inquisitive looks)

"We're umm . . . pregnant."

What inspired me, you ask? Pride. I couldn't stand the idea of them thinking I was benched even for another month before the cat was out of the bag.

Q: Are you already shopping for toddler-sized Riedells?

MD: Soon enough. We've got time for the physicality of skating—which I'm sure will come naturally. Tucker and I are watching all the tournaments now to get up to speed on strategy first.

If worse comes to worst and you just can't live without those long hours of practice and the thrill of competition . . . you can always come back.

After skating for more than two years, Mibbs Breakin' Ribs of the Charm City Roller Girls went back to being just Brandy Hope Busick at the end of 2008. For a while, she enjoyed the extra time she had to do things like laundry and hang out with non-derby pals. But after a while, the joy of free time wore off, she says, "I missed derby like a lost lover. I wanted to be back on the travel team competing so bad."

So Brandy resurrected her derby career. She likens coming back to practice to meeting someone special you haven't seen in a while at the airport, "Your loved one is waiting for you at the end of the terminal, you are nervous and so excited." Though she struggled with endurance practices at first (turns out her return to derby coincided with a case of walking pneumonia!), Mibbs says re-enlisting with her league felt like coming back home.

After retiring, you may find that you enjoy the extra time off and the lack of derby drama, but you really, really miss skating. But perhaps you can't risk a serious injury or don't have the time to commit to derby the way you once did. That's what happened to one woman in Chicago who went on to start a new version of roller derby.

RECREATIONAL ROLLER DERBY

Barbara Dolan, a.k.a. Queen B, was a skater with the Windy City Rollers of Chicago for a little less than two years when she realized she just couldn't keep up with her derby life. Her son got eleven tardies in his first semester of first grade, "because mommy couldn't get her ass out of bed after practices that ended at eleven at night and required a thirty-five minute commute," Queen B recalls. She was also worried about getting hurt. As a forty-four-year old mother of two with a job at a law firm and a three-story house, Queen B knew she'd be S.O.L. if she wound up on crutches.

So she quit derby for a year. But she missed it something fierce. So, she decided to see if she could entice a bunch of gals to skate "just for fun." In November 2007, Queen B led a practice with about a dozen women in attendance. Like that classic Heather Locklear shampoo commercial, those women told their friends, and they told their friends . . . . And before Queen B knew it, she had to cap off her group at forty-two members.

She christened her recreational version of the sport Derby Lite. There are no teams in Derby Lite. Nor are there penalties or referees; skaters abide by the rule of honor, retreating to the back of the pack if they do something naughty, like cutting the track.

Derby Lite skaters use positional blocking instead of the big hits associated with regular derby—Queen B likens it to no-check hockey. And that means skaters in their sixties can and do participate without fear of winding up in the hospital. Derby Lite is also an option for women who are new to the sport and want to learn the basics before trying out for a competing league. Queen B has seen plenty of D'Liters head off to the Windy City Rollers. She says, "I'm the proud mama bird who pouts because her babies have flown the coop."

In the summer of 2009, Barbara's Derby Lite became a licensed business. Similar non-competitive derby groups have taken off in Houston, Austin, Denver, and Los Angeles. Queen B says she thinks rec leagues will play a key role in the future of the sport. "We make roller derby accessible to everyone, no matter your age or ability or time commitment."

When Queen B says Derby Lite is for everyone, she means everyone without a Y chromosome. Like many derby rec leagues, her group is all-girl. But men have also staked a claim in the roller derby revival. As some male skaters put it, "turns out that there *are* balls in derby after all."

MEN'S DERBY

When Sarah "Pink Panza" Lang and her boyfriend Jake "Bazooka Joe" Fahy of Northampton, Massachusetts, decided to launch a league called Pioneer Valley Roller Derby, the couple decided to have divisions for both women and men. By the time Pink Panza and Bazooka Joe secured a place to practice, they had recruited a number of guys and gals. By early 2006, the modern derby revival saw the birth of its first male team—the Dirty Dozen.

They held their first public scrimmage during the half-time of a Charm City Roller Girls game—a scrimmage organized by Charm City ref Justice Feelgood Marshall. "It was just a fifteen minute expo," Justice says, "but it went over so well, and it was so much fun that I knew I had to form a men's team." The Harm City Homicide came to life in 2007. Soon after came the New York Shock Exchange and the Death Quads of Connecticut. Together, these teams formed the Men's Derby Coalition.

There are now several male derby groups including the Quad-fathers in Utica, New York, the Dallas Deception in Texas, and the Whiskey Town Wolfhounds in Tullahoma, Tennessee. Guys are playing derby in the United Kingdom and Australia. Many of these teams abide by WFTDA rules. But with their obvious differences in equipment, men tend to have their own style of play. Matt Dudzic of Baltimore, also known as Virginia Slim of the Harm City Homicide, explains, "Because men tend to be more top-heavy, they usually need to either adopt a wider stance or angle forward slightly more to be stable when blocking."

Men's derby hasn't experienced anything like the explosive growth of the female version of the sport. There are many hypotheses about why this is. Here's one from Justice Feelgood Marshall: female derby players invest a lot more in the public presentation of the sport—everything from uniforms to bout posters. "The guys, it seems, don't care as much about all that, Justice says, "it's more like 'Hey, we've got ten dudes and a floor, let's find ten other dudes and hit them already'."

MEN'S DERBY AT THE NORTHWEST KNOCKDOWN

Virginia Slim says maybe it's because men have plenty of other options when it comes to full-contact sport. Derby ref Howie Swerve once mused that men's derby was doomed to failure. "I know boys," he told Virginia Slim when handed a flyer about men's derby. "We take good ideas from girls and fuck shit up."

After seeing a few bouts, Howie had a change of heart. "Turns out only awesome boys stick around derby," he says. Seems that no matter what your gender, there is something about derby that really brings people together. "At most, if not all, of the bouts we hug each other at the end," says a burly skater known as the Rev. "You won't see the Yankees and Red Sox doing that after a game or going out and having a few beers and just talking to each other," he adds, "that is what is so great about this sport."

Sometimes, skaters of both genders mix it up and form co-ed teams to scrimmage, recalling the pioneer days of derby when Leo Seltzer brought men and women together on teams.

But there's one thing Mr. Seltzer never would have dreamed of . . . kids doing derby!

SEATTLE DERBY BRATS—TINY BUT DEADLY. THE PACIFIC NORTHWEST'S PREMIERE JUNIOR LEAGUE: THE SEATTLE DERBY BRATS, FOUNDED IN 2006; AGES 6-18. FOR MORE INFORMATION GO TO: WWW.SEATTLEDERBYBRATS.COM

JUNIOR DERBY

Around the same time that grown men on the East Coast strapped on skates and started scrimmaging with each other, young girls thousands of miles away in Arizona were doing the same thing.

Dylan Hasman's wife Betsy Hasman (Venus Dynamite) skates with the Tucson Roller Derby, and he would often take his girls, Tristan and Isabelle, to mom's bouts. "My daughters and a number of their friends were big fans and really wanted to *play* roller derby," says Dylan. "So we decided to start training them with the same drills as the adult leagues use." Tristan and Isabelle became Stella Star and Lexie Luthor. And their friends started skating, too—they soon had enough eager, young skaters to form the Tucson Derby Brats—a junior league in the most literal sense.

Featuring many of the daughters of TRD moms, Tuscon launched two divisions—the Derby Brats, for girls ages ten through seventeen, and the Skater Tots, for those between the

A FEW FINAL LAPS

ages of five and nine. They've even been able to get local schools to accept derby for P.E. credit!

Like adult rollergirls, junior skaters enjoy the derby culture—from the fun names to the amazing friendships that bloom during practices. Much like recreational derby, most juniors don't hip check or charge at each other; they rely more on light shoulder blocking and positional blocking. Over the past few years, junior leagues have sprouted up throughout the country, from Seattle, Washington, to Appleton, Wisconsin. Junior derby girls have attended intensive summer camps. They've put together public scrimmages and held inter-league bouts. Young boys have even stepped up to be junior derby referees.

The girls of junior derby are absolutely remarkable. We've had the pleasure of training some of them as part of the L.A. Derby Dolls Junior Dolls program. They pick up the sport quickly, have boundless energy, and rebound from falls faster than many of the best adult skaters.

Like their grown-up counterparts, many junior skaters find the sport provides them with a lot more than something to fill their time after school. "I used to be extremely shy," says Divya Gillespie a.k.a. La Niña, who joined the Tucson Derby Brats when she was thirteen. "With the sisterhood that derby provides, I am much more confident. I think derby creates camaraderie between us girls. After all, we live through pain and joy together and almost seem to complete each other."

Her fellow Derby Brat Arlee Thwing, a.k.a. Effie Bomb, echoes that thought. And, she adds, derby brought her family closer together. Her mom's a retired skater and her dad became a coach with the junior league so they now share a lot in common. "I don't think I'll go to college somewhere where there isn't a league," Effie says, "I want to continue playing derby for as long as I can."

Megan Fabio, a.k.a. MegaBite, also has an eye towards the future. MegaBite started doing derby in L.A. with the Junior Derby Dolls when she was just eleven. Her goals are to become a member of the Dolls' Fight Crew team, and to someday be a Junior Derby trainer herself.

PROFiLE: LUCE BANDIT

Teenager Catherine Bacon is already a roller derby veteran. At age sixteen, she began skating for the Tucson Derby Brats, but last year, between college applications, she was also making derby history as Luc3f3r (pronounced Lucifer). When she was drafted to Tucson Roller Derby's team The Iron Curtain, Luc3f3r became Luce Bandit and the first in what we hope will be a long line of girls to graduate from the junior league to the WFTDA-level big-leagues.

Q: What attracted you to the sport at such a young age?

LUCE BANDIT: It's hard to pinpoint what exactly attracted me to derby initially. The speed was a big part of it, I think. The first bout I went to was a Tucson Roller Derby bout. I'd never heard of derby before. I had no concept of what it was. I went and was hooked almost immediately, though. I knew that I had to do this. Lucky for me, the Tucson Derby Brats were recruiting at that bout. So I took a flyer, showed up at practice the following week, and bought my first pair of skates the next weekend.

Q: Are your parents supportive of your derby career?

LB: They are. They were skeptical at first about whether or not I was going to stick with it. They didn't believe me when

I told them that this was absolutely and without question something I wanted to do. They weren't willing to buy me gear at first, so we worked out a compromise. I told them I was going to do this no matter what and that I would buy my own skates if that was what it took. But, since I was pretty much broke, I only had enough money for the skates themselves, not pads as well. So the deal was this: I bought my skates, my parents bought the protective gear. They definitely support me, though. They come to my bouts and cheer me on, which is great.

Q: If a young girl was thinking about joining junior derby, what are some of the things you would tell her to expect?

LB: I would tell her to expect to have fun. And that yes, you fall. When you're new, sometimes a lot. But that's okay. What's important is that you keep getting up again. There's so much personal strength associated with derby, I think. It pushes you to push yourself in ways you didn't know you could.

Q: Have you found that your experience in the sport has affected the way you approach things in your non-derby life?

LB: Definitely. I used to be a more introverted, quiet person. I think derby helped me come out of my shell. Though I'm still fairly quiet, I've definitely gotten louder, which is a good thing, in my opinion.

Q: What are some of the differences you've found in moving up to the WFTDA level?

LB: You can't rely on strength or power in the Brats since you aren't allowed to hit, so you are forced to gain position on opposing skaters instead. So, clearly, hitting was a big difference. It took a little bit to remember to watch for people setting up to hit me, because that wasn't a habit I had acquired skating with the Brats.

Q: When you graduated to WFTDA level derby, were your new teammates, the Iron Curtain, supportive?

LB: They were wonderful. The captain and co-captain worked with me to help me adjust to the hitting aspect, which basically meant I was the punching bag for several drills, ha, ha. Seriously, though, it was great training. I learned quickly and even enjoyed it. I had a great season with the Iron Curtain, and I really enjoyed skating with them.

Q: How do you think that the growing Junior Derby enrollment will ultimately affect the sport of roller derby?

LB: I think it will have some interesting effects. Because junior skaters are young, they pick up skills easily. I think junior leagues will graduate some amazing and experienced skaters. At the same time, though, for that same reason, it could at some point down the road make it more difficult for women, most of whom haven't skated since they were kids, to join as adults. Maybe. Who knows? I think one thing that will certainly come of it is waves of young, skilled, experienced skaters, which will perpetuate the sport's growth.

Q: So, you've just started college this fall. Will you continue skating?

LB: I'm attending the University of Texas at Austin. When I was applying for school, though, the Texas Roller Girls were actually a 21+ league. They voted and changed their age policy to 18+ about a month before I moved to Austin for school. I definitely plan to keep doing derby. Frankly, I'm not sure what I would do without derby. It's hard to imagine.

Luc3f3r joined the Texas Rollergirls as soon as she arrived in Austin. She has been making great strides as her new incarnation, Luce Bandit, one of the Hell Marys' go-to jammers. She is the youngest skater in the history of the veteran league.

WILL DERBY LAST?

When you see an eight-year-old in a pair of well-worn skates talking about the rush of jamming through a pack, it's hard not to feel a rush of exhilaration and optimism about this sport. We dream of a day when roller derby will be part of the standard high school gym curriculum . . . or maybe even part of the Olympics!

But this wouldn't be the first time that skaters had high hopes for the sport only to watch it vanish into the ether. In the fall of 1972, more than 52,000 fans turned out for a match between the Midwest Pioneers and the L.A. T-birds in Chicago's Comiskey Park. Back then it probably seemed certain that the sport was here to stay forever . . . But it didn't turn out that way.

Even as recently as 2001, skepticism for roller derby's longevity abounded. *Hell on Wheels* documentarian Bob Ray remembers the climate in Austin before BGGW held their debut bout. "Nobody even thought they would do it," he laughs, "People ridiculed us for even bothering to film it."

Even many of the skaters themselves once believed at best, derby would survive, but never grow beyond the Lone Star State. "Some thought derby would never leave Austin," says one of the pioneers of this current incarnation, Sparkle Plenty. "But always from the start, I thought this would be huge." So far, Sparkle is right.

No one knows where this modern incarnation of derby is headed from here. We're smart enough not to make any predictions ourselves. But we will confess this—there are days when we worry. We wonder if conflicting notions about the future of the sport will spark dangerous rifts among the derby community. We fear what might happen if, as it has in the past, television comes calling and morphs derby into a commercialized product, devoid of the spirit that gave birth to its current incarnation. We dread that derby has jumped the proverbial shark when the national retail outlet Hot Topic launches a "Roller Derby Queen" line featuring photos of bruise-free models and not a single skate in sight. "You won't have to battle it out on the rink to sport some killer Roller Derby fashion," the ad promises.

Sigh.

But then we get an e-mail from a *real* rollergirl. Her name is Twilight in the Zone, and she explains why she skates. Yeah, she digs the clothes and the make-up. She loves the friends she's made. But the most important reason she loves roller derby—the skating. "I love the feeling of going at what seems a million miles an hour, finding holes," she writes. "I also love how focused my whole body is in holding back and blocking someone else, of communicating with my team, especially when the result is a fluidly changing pack, or a rock steady wall in the front. And when else, really, do girls get to slam their whole bodies into *another* body?"

Twilight is fourteen. Skaters like her make us feel confident that derby is here to stay for a good long while.

CALLING OFF THIS JAM

There's a roller derby anthem, a rockabilly song called "Roller Derby Saved My Soul" by a guy named Leon Chase. In 2007, Chase's band, Uncle Leon and the Alibis, produced the tune and what became a very popular line of t-shirts, pins, and undies to go with it. The title, Leon says, means different things to different people.

To us, it means that there are some phenomenal chapters in our lives that never would have happened had we not become derby girls.

For Kasey, it meant co-captaining the original Tru$t Fund Terrors team (the greatest bunch of girls anyone could ever hope to skate with). It meant finding the courage and support to come out to her family. Derby provided her the honor of being featured in *The Advocate* magazine. There's also body checking Chris Pontius in an episode of *Wild Boys*, and meeting welcoming women all over the country while traveling for the league.

For Axles, it meant co-captaining the original Tough Cookies team. (And she would beg to differ with Kasey here—Axles's team totally kicked the TFT's asses!). Doing derby also meant discovering that she could go from barely being able to cross over at the rink to being able to drop in on a half-pipe at the skate park. There was also the time she skated on Fifth Avenue with Drew Barrymore and the Gotham Girls on CBS's *Early Morning Show*. There was the honor of having rollergirls as ushers at her wedding and her derby wife, Kitty Scratch, serving as her maven of honor.

For all the things we've done together, well, some history is just better told over a couple of beers . . . . Of course, roller derby also gave us the amazing opportunity to write this, our very first book.

We hope you've enjoyed reading it. But more than that, we hope it's whet your derby appetite—whether that means starting your own league, or sticking around for another season, going to your first bout or becoming a die hard slave to your local league. Time to see how derby can save your soul.

NORTH STAR ROLLERGIRL HOPEFUL SLY JINX SIGNS UP FOR TRYOUTS BEFORE MAKING THE TEAM

THIS COULD BE YOU.

DOWN AND DERBY

APPENDIX: DERBY IN FILM AND TELEVISION

THE REAL LIFE characters you've read about in this book so far are the stuff of screenwriters' dreams. These people are larger than life, volatile, and charismatic. Between the personas and the theatrical action of the sport itself, it's no surprise that derby's had a recurring role in film and TV over the years.

Ever since 1946, when a short film called *Roller Derby Girl* was nominated for an Academy Award, derby has enjoyed media attention both scripted and unscripted. Actors and genuine competitors alike have brought the sport to life on the screen. Skaters have done everything from portraying a roller derby dog to skating circles around Katie Couric. They've eaten bacon with Brian Boitano and appeared in a video with The Breeders.

If we were to tell you about every appearance of the sport or its athletes in the media, we'd have to leave breadcrumbs to find our way out of the mountain of footage. So instead, in this section, we'd like to turn the projector on to view some of the ways derby has appeared in feature-length films and documentaries and guest-starred in scripted television shows over the years.

FILM

THE FIREBALL (1950)
DIRECTOR: Tay Garnett
WRITERS: Tay Garnett, Horace McCoy
CAST: Mickey Rooney, Pat O'Brien, Beverly Tyler, Milburn Stone, Glen Corbett, Marilyn Monroe

PLOT SYNOPSIS: In 1950, roller derby was the hottest thing on television. *The Fireball* aimed to take that action to the big screen—and it did, in spades. Though hardly remembered as a classic of cinema today, *The Fireball* is actually a terrific slice of derby action—both progressive in its portrayal of women and in its insistence on a protagonist that is not always sympathetic.

Mickey Rooney plays Johnny Casar, an orphan with a Napoleon complex, who escapes the kindly clutches of Father O'Hara's home to try his luck in the world. That luck introduces him to a pair of discarded metal strap-on skates, which, in turn, introduces the audience to a series of comical pratfalls.

In order to gain control of his wobbly strides, he heads for the local rink where national co-ed speed skating champions Mack and Mary offer lessons for free. While Mack proves to be a bit of a douche bag, Mary sees something in Johnny that she likes. She takes him under her wing and teaches him to be a champion skater just like herself. Next step—roller derby.

After Johnny finally manages to beat Mack at a no-rules match race, he demands membership on the derby squad. Feeding off his new-found popularity, Johnny becomes a tiny terror—a spotlight vampire who values teamwork about as much as John Holmes values abstinence. And you know the price selfish bastards pay in derby, right? That's right—they get polio! Wait . . . what!?! Don't worry, though, it's a "mild case." Johnny will have a chance to redeem his errant ways . . . but will he?

BEST DERBY MOMENT: Sure, it might be 1950, but this is still roller derby. Though the film admirably never mentions the unconventionality of a woman teaching a man how to play sports, Mary is unquestionably the expert coach. After Johnny has lost several match races to Mack, Mary teaches him how to take a hit by throwing a few of her own. At one point, she tosses him a shoulder so decisive that he hits the ground stunned. But rather than getting angry, Johnny simply beams and says, "Wonderful!"

WORST DERBY MOMENT: No one likes a showboater—especially when it threatens the safety of the team. As Johnny becomes more popular, his motto becomes, "Things happen Johnny's way or people get hurt." He puts this into practice when he sends his own teammate flying over the rail rather than letting him score in the jam. And somewhere out there, a modern ref just read that sentence and suffered his first derby-related seizure.

FUN FACT: The character of Johnny Casar is mostly based on the life and trials of an actual skater. Eddie Poore skated for the International Roller Speedway—a renegade competitor of Leo Seltzer's Roller Derby that toured Europe and the Philippines from 1937 through the 1950s—under the name Eddie Cazar. Like Johnny, Eddie's star skating career was nearly decimated by the onset of polio. Unlike in the film, where polio looks about as serious as hay fever, Cazar went through agonizing treatment to regain his health before he was able to once again put on skates. Where the film treats polio as a bold morality lesson, Cazar's real story is one of triumph and determination to beat the odds.

KANSAS CITY BOMBER (1972)
DIRECTOR: Jerrold Freedman
WRITERS: Calvin Clements Sr., Thomas Rickman
CAST: Raquel Welch, Kevin McCarthy, Helena Kallianiotes,
Norman Alden, Jeanne Cooper, Jodie Foster

PLOT SYNOPSIS: Raquel Welch plays single mother Diane "KC" Carr, a Roller Games skater who finds herself traded from Kansas City to Portland after losing a high-stakes match race. Skating in Portland puts her closer to her two children, now cared for by their grandmother, but her single-minded focus on the sport still provides a hearty block against traditional motherhood. New league owner Mr. Henry, however, has no question about KC's allure—both as a potential roller star and as a potential lover. KC's budding affair with Mr. Henry does nothing to endear her to her teammates.

Former star and current budding alcoholic Jackie Burdette decides she's worked too hard to let an attractive face and (let's admit, a *wow*!) figure topple her from the top of the roster. Tensions mount on the team until KC is forced to gamble her team position in another harrowing match race. Unlike the same year's *Unholy Rollers*, *Kansas City Bomber* aims to play it straight, emphasizing downbeat drama over fever pitched action.

BEST DERBY MOMENT: An amazingly illegal, but nonetheless acrobatic, do-si-do defensive whip between opponents Judy Sowinski and Jackie Burdette. As a result, Jackie slams the rail harder than she slams her whiskey.

WORST DERBY MOMENT—OR—WORST PERFORMANCE BY A PAIR OF WIGS: In the final match race between KC and Jackie, all the hard-hitting action is clearly performed by doubles. How do you know this? Because their hair somehow always manages to cover their faces in a tangled curtain that could send Cousin It into a fit of jealousy.

FUN FACT: Roller Games star Judy Arnold not only served as Raquel Welch's skating advisor on the film, but she was also the fleet-footed skater hiding beneath that terrible wig in all the hard-hitting action sequences. Roller Games fans might revel in seeing Arnold and real-life archrival Judy Sowinski skating as teammates. Modern derby fans might know Sowinski as one of the coaches of the Penn-Jersey She Devils.

UNHOLY ROLLERS (1972)
DIRECTOR: Vernon Zimmerman
WRITER: Howard R. Cohen
CAST: Claudia Jennings, Candice Roman, Betty Ann Rees, Alan Vint, Roberta Collins, Kathleen Freeman

PLOT SYNOPSIS: Playboy Playmate of the Year 1970, Claudia Jennings, plays Karen Walker, a severely disgruntled employee at a cat food factory. Her boss, a smarmy poster boy for sexual harassment, sends the feisty employee clawing for the exit. When she hears about tryouts for the local roller derby, she figures that her hair-trigger temper and colorful vocabulary will make her a shoo-in for this new career choice—never mind her questionable skate skills. With the support of her roommate and her roommate's larcenous boyfriend, Karen's tryouts are a rousing success. She'll be skating as the newest member of the L.A. Avengers! But while the audience may love Karen's fiery "showmanship," the Avengers' current star, Micki, is no fan after her Sapphic charms are rebuffed by the newbie. Karen soon learns it's a rough and lonely road to the victory lap, and that the fingers you skate over on the way up aren't likely to lend you an assist on the way down. Jennings' extreme, hard-boiled delivery and a gritty, B-movie feel put *Unholy Rollers* in a league of its own.

BEST DERBY MOMENT: Karen gets drummed off the track by her teammates, but maniacally takes the derby action right into the street. In a near-deadly blocking game with a giant sedan, she nonetheless flashes her trademark Avengers forearm tattoo in triumph. Classic.

WORST DERBY MOMENT: An on-the-track love scene between Karen and her smarmy, married teammate Nick Vanitas. It's entirely plausible, though, that Karen was just making a valiant attempt to get him out of a horrible poufy American flag shirt that made him look more like Brandi than Brando. In which case, we're inclined to forgive her, with apologies.

FUN FACT: *Unholy Rollers* was edited by Martin Scorsese under heavy coercion from Roger Corman. At the time, Scorsese was busy with another little project you may have heard of—*Mean Streets*.

THE SHAGGY D.A. (1976)
DIRECTOR: Robert Stevenson
WRITERS: Don Tait, Felix Salten
CAST: Dean Jones, Tim Conway, Suzanne Pleshette, Keenan Wynn, Dick Van Patten

PLOT SYNOPSIS: In the sequel to Walt Disney's *The Shaggy Dog*, Dean Jones takes the role of Wilby Daniels, a man with the misfortune of transforming into a wooly mutt at the most inopportune moments. In *The Shaggy D.A.*, the magic ring responsible for the hair-raising nightmare in the first film has been safely encased in a museum display. No longer worried that his doggy style will "ruff" up his life, Daniels has become a successful lawyer running for district attorney. When thieves steal the ring and sell it to a bumbling roller derby-loving ice cream man played by Tim Conway, things go to the hounds once again. Madcap antics include a derby bout, the classic pie fight, and a cast of '70s characters that reads like a who's who of funny "Hey! It's that guy!"

BEST DERBY MOMENT: Wilby, as a shaggy mutt, disguises himself as a female roller derby skater and takes a massive airborne whip. If you think that talking animals are funny, wait until you see a person in a bad bipedal dog costume jamming in full derby gear! Woof indeed!

WORST DERBY MOMENT: See above.

FUN FACT: If you look carefully, you can spot several members of the L.A. T-Birds team on the track in the derby scene, including the legendary Gwen "Skinny Minnie" Miller. Skinny Minnie was both a schoolteacher and a derby superstar in the seventies Roller Games heyday, and if you're lucky, you can still get pointers from the still-active skater today.

DEMON OF THE DERBY (2001)
DIRECTOR: Sharon Rutter
CAST: Ann Calvello, Jerry Seltzer, Jan Vallow, Teri Ann Conte

PLOT SYNOPSIS: This documentary explores the amazing life of Ann Calvello—"The Meanest Mama on Skates." Ann began her derby career in 1948 and went on to skate for six decades. A true maverick on wheels, she was known for her brightly colored punk-rock hairdos, humongous earrings, and outrageous style.

Demon of the Derby includes archival footage showing Ann in her glory days when she happily earned a reputation as a feisty villain who frequently throttled competitors with her towel. Modern footage shows Ann during a brief stint with the American Roller Derby as a member of the Demons team. We also see her off-skates in her apartment, filled with stuffed animal lions (Ann was a very proud Leo) and in later jobs as a grocery store bagger and a ticket taker at San Francisco '49er games.

Demon of the Derby also depicts Ann's experience on the receiving end of hurt—and not just multiple broken bones (she earned the nickname Banana Nose for a reason). We learn that she grew up with an abusive father and went on to marry an abusive husband. We meet Teri Ann Conte, the distant daughter Ann left behind as she skated around the world. And we share her heartbreak when Ann's ousted from the American Roller Derby League in her senior years. The skaters say they're worried about hurting a senior citizen like Ann, but it also seems as if some of the other women of the league want their chance to be shining stars.

This film not only captures the spirit of one of America's most outrageous athletes but also provides a thoughtful illustration of how the sport of derby has morphed over time.

BEST DERBY MOMENT: When Ann was seventy-one years old, she gets invited to participate in the *RollerJam* TV show. She travels to Florida and participates in a match race with skater Kenneth Loge III, who is easily less than half her age. Before the big event,

DOWN AND DERBY

Ann gets frightfully nervous because she hasn't skated in two years. But in the end, she pulls it off! With a trademark Calvello knee to the backside maneuver, she beats her opponent in the home stretch!

WORST DERBY MOMENT: After being booted from the American Derby League, Ann shows up to a game. Her former colleague Jan Vallow is presented with a lifetime achievement award while Ann sits in the bleachers empty-handed, her dark sunglasses hiding the tears. It's a terrible insult—one of many times Ann felt slighted by the sport she loved so.

FUN FACT: The episode of *RollerJam* that Ann skated in was the last one that ever aired.

To help raise money to make this documentary, Ann donated a bunch of her personal items and derby memorabilia to be auctioned. The item that got the highest bid was one of her bras. "It was an impressive one," says *Demon of the Derby* producer Christine Murray, "pointy and black-laced and as I recall, a 36-DD."

JAM (2006)
DIRECTOR: Mark Woollen
CAST: Tim Patten, Dan Ferrari, Alfonso Reyes, Larry Lee, Pam Schwab, Karey Marengo, Stacey Blitsch

PLOT SYNOPSIS: "In 1973 Roller Derby died . . . Nobody told them." That's the tag line for this excellent documentary that follows seven years' worth of unsuccessful attempts by the American Roller Derby League to revive the old-school version of the sport in northern California.

The story revolves around Tim Patten, a former skater who is diagnosed HIV positive in 1983. Patten is utterly obsessed with roller derby—he says it's what keeps him alive. He manages a motley group of skaters who've been doing derby for decades. They have strong wills but broken bodies and skates that are barely held together with duct tape. Take for example IceBox—the 450-pound skater who's been at it for more than twenty-one years. "I'm kind of out of shape," he admits while his mammoth gut drips into his lap, "But if I can get in tip-top shape, the league can go far . . . ." Or not.

These folks are desperate to relive the fame they enjoyed during derby's pinnacle in the sixties and seventies. Over meetings at Round Table Pizza, they fantasize about sell-out crowds. But in reality, few fans turn up and the skaters wind up earning a mere $25 per game. Guys like Alfonso Reyes and Larry Lee—once young, agile competitors—drink hard liquor out of the trunk of the car and chain-smoke before bouts.

When they do take to the banked track, it's a very different version of derby—all spectacle and little sport. "The premise of the game is not skating," Patten declares, "the premise of the game is a grudge." The American Roller Derby League skaters script out their games in advance and spend a good chunk of the game bickering with audience members and throwing folding chairs at their rivals. Patten even goes so far as to try and stir racial drama between black, white, and Hispanic skaters.

This documentary is hilarious at moments. But these people lead hard lives both on and off the track—this is not a feel-good flick. *Jam* definitely offers some excellent insight into the roller derby of yesteryear.

BEST DERBY MOMENT: At the very end of the film, we see Tim Patten at a TXRD Lonestar Rollergirls game in Austin. As he watches this new version of derby come to life in front of a huge, enthusiastic audience, you can catch a glimmer in his eye. It looks as if he feels his efforts were truly worth it after all.

WORST DERBY MOMENT: At one of the league's infamous pizza meetings, Tim is trying to convince Pam Schwab, a newer skater, to join the villainous Demons team. Pam resists—she wants to be a heroine, to have the crowd beg for her autograph. Trying to convince her to go to the dark side, Tim says, "When you become a star it's not because of your skills, it's because of who you invented in your mind." To the women who work hard to make this sport legit today, that line is like a swift kick in the gut.

FUN FACT: One of the bonus features of the DVD is "A Day With Ann Calvello." It's great footage of "the meanest mama on skates" that the director couldn't use because Ann had just stopped skating with the American Roller Derby League when he shot it. Calvello introduces us to her cats, and her Avon lady and shares this gem about her choice of cosmetics: "I never wore dark lipstick in my life because my mouth looks like a baboon's ass when I put it on!"

HELL ON WHEELS (2007)
DIRECTOR: Bob Ray, Produced by Werner Campbell
CAST: The original members of Bad Girl, Good Woman Productions and the Texas Rollergirls

PLOT SYNOPSIS: In 2001, roller derby was recreated in Austin, Texas, by a group of tenacious and not always like-minded women. Documentarians Bob Ray and Werner Campbell were there filming it all.

The film begins by following the newly formed BGGW as they create a brand new form of roller derby for the millennium and train for their first public bouts. As the film progresses, however, Ray and Campbell begin to turn their eye to the personality conflicts and cracks in the She-E-Os leadership that would cause the league to undergo a painful split.

For a comprehensive overview of Austin's trials and tribulations to become the First City of Modern Roller Derby, see Chapter Four. For a live-action lesson in the challenges of maintaining peace amongst several dozen strong-willed, intelligent, and opinionated women, see *Hell on Wheels*. And remember—Texas went through the hard stuff so those who followed wouldn't have to.

BEST DERBY MOMENT: Ray and Campbell give us something that is rare and precious in this documentary—a chance to see the first modern roller derby bout in action. It is not often that you are able to see a phenomenon being born, but *Hell on Wheels* takes you right into the derby delivery room. The thousands of bouts that have followed in the wake of this first one were all based on the excitement and awe you see in the skaters' faces when they realize that, yep, they're really pulling this off!

WORST DERBY MOMENT: In the first bout the Lonestar Rollergirls hold after the split, skater Cha Cha suffers a nearly unwatchable injury. As she slips, her leg meets the kick rail, and breaks literally in half mid-shin. If you missed it in the real-time coverage, Ray and Campbell repeat all the gory, unnaturally rubbery detail in extra slow motion.

FUN FACT: Filming the infamous leg break was even more difficult than watching it. During filming, Bob Ray says, "I'm filming Cha Cha as her fishnet is getting cut away—blood squirting everywhere. I'm about to pass out thinking, 'This is horrible, this is f'ing grotesque!'" Meanwhile, Rhinestone Cowgirls skater Lux, who is a nurse, skates up to him and notices that he's looking a little peaked. "She says, 'Maybe you should sit down,'" Ray remembers. "And I'm like, 'Yeah, I think I've got enough of this.'" But for anyone wondering how Cha Cha felt about the footage, Ray assures us that she was its biggest fan. "I'm pretty sure she showed it to more people than we ever did—she was proud of it!"

Eight years after the split, the Texas Rollergirls and the Lonestar Rollergirls still have not skated against each other in a bout. However, time has cooled much of the crosstown rivalry. Recently, skaters have rolled together at practices, and discussions have been on the table for a match-up in the near future.

BLOOD ON THE FLAT TRACK (2008)
DIRECTORS: Lainy Bagwell and Lacy Levitt
CAST: The Rat City Rollergirls

FAMILY FEUD—DEE BOMB OF RAT CITY'S DERBY LIBERATION FRONT DRAGS HER REAL-LIFE SISTER FEMME FATALE TO THE GROUND.

PHOTO BY MICHAEL COYOTE

PLOT SYNOPSIS: This film highlights the rise of the Rat City Rollergirls from an ambitious bunch of disparate skaters to one of the most powerful forces in modern derby. Bagwell and Levitt have created a documentary that is a true insider's view of what it takes to operate a successful flat track league, highlighting not just the game play and business structure, but also the individual and wildly interesting characters that make up the league's four teams. By focusing tightly on Rat City's bid for derby dominance, the film manages along the way to personalize the universal derby experience.

BEST DERBY MOMENT: *Blood on the Flat Track* shows a great knack for exposing the more tender side of the Rat pack, and in doing so also becomes the first film to let derby out of the closet. It has long been common knowledge among the derby cognoscenti that the sport has a rich tradition of embracing its homosexual competitors, but publicly only in a sort of military "don't ask, don't tell" manner. Bagwell and Levitt operate under no such pretenses, and allow the viewer the opportunity to briefly share in derby love of all stripe—mother/daughter (Miss Fortune and

Hot Flash, Lorna Boom coaching with her baby in her arms), announcer/skater marriage (Jake Stratton and Clobberin' Mame), sibling support (the Tomaccio sisters—Dee Bomb, Femme Fatale, and Blonde An'Bitchin), and on-track rivals/off-track partners (Burnett Down and Basket Casey, Shovey Chase and Kitty Kamikaze)—with equal doses of hilarity and sweetness.

WORST DERBY MOMENT: Fans of the Rat City Rollergirls may be disappointed that footage of the gals' dominance of the 2007 West Coast Regionals in Tucson was not included. It would have been great to see Rat City finally take on the then-unbeatable Texas Rollergirls and win.

FUN FACT: Basket Casey and her unself-conscious wit are without a doubt a highlight of the film. Not only did Lainy Bagwell have the opportunity to get personal with Casey in the interviews, but she once accidentally got personal on the track. The director says, "The scene where Basket Casey (who is my favorite for obvious reasons) slams into the camera was a real hit on me. I wasn't worried about protecting myself when she came flying at me. Instead, I instinctually grabbed my camera and hugged it to me." Footage shows what Basket Casey can do to a blocker—one can only imagine what she could do to a helplessly delicate piece of photo equipment!

WHIP IT! (2009)
DIRECTOR: Drew Barrymore
WRITER: Shauna Cross
CAST: Ellen Page, Drew Barrymore, Juliette Lewis, Kristin Wiig, Eve, Zoe Bell, Ari Graynor, Jimmy Fallon, Andrew Wilson, Rachel Piplica, Kristen Adolfi

PLOT SUMMARY: Based on a young adult novel written by retired L.A. Derby Doll Shauna Cross (a.k.a. the real Maggie Mayhem), Ellen Page stars as Bliss Cavendar. Bliss is a restless teen from Bodeen, Texas, who is force-fed a beauty pageant lifestyle by her well-meaning mom. On a trip to Austin, Bliss sees a rowdy pack of roller skaters enter a boutique. Intrigued, she picks up one of their flyers. "Roller Derby!!" it professes in bold letters. Disguised as sudden boosters of their high school football squad, Bliss and her B.F.F. Pash slip out of town to see the banked track derby action in Austin. Bliss is hooked. An offer from team captain Maggie Mayhem and a challenge by Pash inspires Bliss to dig out her old Barbie skates, lie about her age, and give tryouts a shot.

Though wobbly at first, Bliss quickly catches on. The ingénue is drafted to the last place team, the Hurl Scouts, and is rechristened Babe Ruthless. Along with fellow new teammates—a brutish pair of deaf former hockey players called, indistinguishably, the Manson Sisters—the Hurl Scouts try to improve their notorious losing streak. Standing in their way are the vicious Holy Rollers led by bully veteran Iron Maven (Juliette Lewis).

Along the way, Bliss faces the challenges of skater envy, non-derby friends feeling abandoned, falling in love for the first time, and the perils of lying to a mother who strongly disproves of the sport.

BEST DERBY MOMENT: This is the first (and we certainly hope not the last) feature film to depict modern roller derby. And they cast real derby girls to fill most of the skater roles. Seeing real skaters, from the petite and thoroughly pierced Kat Von Destroya to the wonderful wall of woman known as Whiskey, doing their thing on the big screen is a tremendous thrill.

But, one of our favorite derby moments of this film actually happens off-skates. When Bliss tries to describe why she derbies to her disapproving mother, she declares that she's fallen in love . . . with the sport of derby. She is so passionate that legions of understanding derby girls will quickly reach for a tissue.

WORST DERBY MOMENT: Okay, so time for a disclaimer. Both of us worked on the film, training the actresses and supervising the skating. Needless to say, we're a little biased here, especially knowing how hard everyone worked on the movie. For us, the worst moment is one you won't see in the film. Ellen Page trained for months before the shoot and fell in love with derby. Though her role is a jammer, she also loved blocking.

One afternoon we were shooting a scene where another actress took on the role of Hurl Scout jammer and Ellen eagerly volunteered to fill out the roster of blockers. During the jam she fell into the infield and landed on her wrist, howling in pain. Standing on the infield, we feared the worst. But a few moments later, much like the trooper she plays in the film, Ellen got up and shook off the injury, to the applause of several hundred extras. Mother hens that we are, we never let her block again for the remainder of the shoot.

FUN FACT: One scene features a messy food fight with four of the teams. When they were filming, no one bothered to tell the novice actresses playing the Manson Sisters they shouldn't actually eat their chili each time, since they'd be doing multiple takes. Both reported not feeling so well by the end of the night.

Everyone in the cast and crew definitely got into the derby vibe. Many picked their own derby names, such as Guy Bitchie and Pillsbury Ho-Boy. Some even formed mini-teams based on their profession. The hair folks became the *Hot Rollers* and the make-up team dubbed themselves the *Powder Puffs*.

PROFILE: ELLEN "BABE RUTHLESS" PAGE

PHOTO BY DARREN MICHAELS, COURTESY OF FOX SEARCHLIGHT

Q: When you first got involved with Whip It!, what were your thoughts on roller derby?

ELLEN PAGE: I didn't know much about roller derby and I wasn't completely aware of the resurgence that was occurring. I was mostly familiar with the Raquel Welch, seventies theatrical wrestling version. So that's what came to my brain and the thought of that was incredibly exciting.

And then I read the script, and I was looking into this modern resurgence of roller derby and was completely infatuated. When I went to my first L.A. Derby Dolls game with Drew Barrymore, I was just blown away. Blown away.

Q: What about it blew you away?

EP: First and foremost, it's the athleticism, and it's the fact that although there's this extremely theatrical kind of fun with the costumes and names, there are incredibly strong women for no money at all going out there and playing this game and loving it! And they're able to be aggressive and strong and a little bit violent and it's okay.

To be able to watch that is empowering and inspiring and to me is like nothing that exists right now. It's like watching no other sport. There's nothing more exciting than watching a derby game.

Q: What was it like when you actually strapped skates on and starting doing derby yourself?

EP: Learning derby at first was, of course, intimidating, because I remember going to the game and getting so excited to learn this but also being scared shitless, thinking—how am I going to be able to do this? I really wanted to do everything called for in the movie, but am I really going to be able to do this at the end of a couple of months?

It was intimidating, but I always played sports when I was a kid so I love being able to throw my body into something and being able to push myself. Being able to feel that again was really thrilling. And I just worked hard and had the privilege of being able to take the time to learn.

Q: Most derby skaters today play on a flat track. What was it like skating on that banked surface?

EP: Intimidating. Because, even before I started skating on the track, you have to learn how to get on the track; how to get off; how to feel comfortable on the highest part of the track . . . And all of those things that become second nature eventually are really frightening at first.

And then it's funny because it's become so second nature that when I'm skating on a flat surface it feels strange to me. Recently I was in a roller rink for fun but it felt like something was missing because you don't have that bank.

Q: *Bliss's skate name was Babe Ruthless. And on set Drew called you Small Newman in reference to Paul Newman in* Slapshot. *But you came up with another derby name of your own . . . .*

EP: Hurt Vonnegut. Because I'm a massive Kurt Vonnegut fan.

Q: *What effect do you think roller derby had on the character you played—a Texas teen named Bliss Cavendar?*

EP: What I think is exciting about this is that you have a girl who's not exactly being forced into beauty pageants, but it's not something that's igniting a passionate fire in her. And thus, there's a shy quality to her, she's introverted and not incredibly confident.

Then when she discovers this other world, literally her blood starts to boil and this passion leads to a confidence that leads to overall strength and wholeness and groundedness in every aspect of her life. And I think that's what it would be like for anyone finding her passion—whether it's roller derby or whether it's filmmaking or goodness knows what it could be. . . . It could be beauty pageants. It's just whatever that thing is that we fall in love with that instills us with confidence to live up to our potential. Because we all have, as cheesy as it sounds, that power within us. It's just about finding it and embracing it and bringing it out.

That's why I think roller derby is so exciting for young women. With the gender stereotypes, you're not encouraged to be strong, to have a strong body even. There's the media saturation of what a young girl should be and it's so tiresome and it causes girls to be so pigeonholed and the derby world is so good to foster strength in girls.

TELEVISION

THE ADDAMS FAMILY: "THE ROLLER DERBY STORY" (1973)
Season 1, Episode 14
DIRECTOR: Charles A. Nichols
WRITERS: Bud Atkinson, Charles Addams, David Levy, Dick Conway, Gene Thompson
CAST: Jackie Coogan, Janet Waldo, Ted Cassidy, Leonard Weinrib

PLOT SYNOPSIS: This is an awesome episode of the Hanna-Barbera animated version of *The Addams Family*. The family's gothic mansion is now a haunted RV that comes with its own hovering dark cloud and piranha-filled moat. For daughter Wednesday's birthday, they travel to the Roller Palace to see a bout between the Demons and the Angels. True to form, the Demons are a bunch of rolling rapscallions led by Pete the Cheat. They trounce the beloved Angels, featuring a lollipop-loving Shirley Templeton. Adding insult to injury, the Demons sabotage the Angels' travel bus before they all head to the world championship game in Los Angeles.

The Addams family have so much fun at the bout, they decide to head to L.A. to watch the big battle. Along the way, they come across the Angels and their broken-down bus. The Addams Family invites the Angels skaters to join them on board their terror-filled trailer. The skaters appreciate the lift but that night they get so creeped out by the ghoulish family that they jump off the spook-mobile, leaving only the Angels' coach behind.

The Addams family feels terribly guilty about frightening off the team, so they decide to fill in for the Angels skaters. At first they can barely stand up on roller skates, and the Demons quickly rack up points. But the Addams skaters eventually get the hang of it and soon develop some amazing strategies. They use plays that could only come to life through animation (including one with a skating octopus!). In the end, the underdogs win and the Angels invite the Addams Family to become permanent members of their team.

BEST DERBY MOMENT: During the championship bout, Morticia dispatches their pet vulture to send a strategy called the Tower of Pizza to Gomez on the track. In this play, Uncle Fester leaps onto Lurch's shoulders, then Gomez flies onto Fester's shoulders, and Granny climbs aboard Gomez's shoulders. They all lean over, becoming an arch that curls over the wall formed by the dreaded Demons. Then the two Addams kids skate up and over their kin to earn a boatload of points.

WORST DERBY MOMENT: En route to the big game, Uncle Fester tells the kids about his days as a skater for the Transylvania Tarantulas. He gets tripped up on his skates and winds up draped on a clothesline, his bald pate peaking out of the crap-hole of a union suit. Fester declares, "In skating, you have to be good at finding openings!"

FUN FACT: The voice of Pugsley Addams was none other than a then eight-year old Jodie Foster.

CHARLIE'S ANGELS: "ANGELS ON WHEELS" (1976)
Season 1, Episode 12
DIRECTOR: Richard Benedict
STORY BY: Charles Sailor
STARRING: Farrah Fawcett, Kate Jackson, Jaclyn Smith

PLOT SYNOPSIS: Karen Jason is the beautiful blonde star of the Tornadoes derby team. During a heated game against the rival Satans, Karen's given a forceful whip by team captain Bad Betty that sends her over the railing. When Karen hits the floor, a brutish thug named Jeremy snaps her neck, killing her. Despite the crowds standing within inches of the incident, no one seems to notice the murderer's obvious move. Her death is labeled a roller games "accident."

Soon after, Charlie's Angel Jill (Farrah Fawcett) is called upon to go undercover as Karen's sister, Barbara. As she learns the ropes of roller derby, Jill also discovers an elaborate insurance scheme. Posing as Barbara, she tries to get in on the action. Meanwhile her fellow Angels Sabrina and Kelly do some detective work, posing as an insurance inspector and a woman's magazine writer.

The bad guys eventually figure out what's going on and decide to get rid of Barbara the same way they did her sister Karen. Once again, Betty provides a powerful whip that sends Barbara over the rail. But this time, the foul play is thwarted! Charlie's Angels are there for back up and save the day.

BEST DERBY MOMENT: After narrowly escaping death, Jill tells the other Angels she has some unfinished business. Even though her job as a private investigator is through, her derby duties remain. She hops back on the track and waits for Bad Betty. With Kelly and Sabrina egging her on, Jill elbows her in the face, drops her to the track, knees her in the gut and pile drives her in the back before giddily declaring, "Charlie told me I'd be a big hit on skates!!"

WORST DERBY MOMENT: When Jill first signs on posing as Barbara, she meets the Tornadoes' owner Hugh Morris (played by Dick Sargent, known best as Darren in that other classic show *Bewitched*). Morris asks if he can look her over. Eager to impress, Jill readily complies and playing off his other occupation as a car dealer shimmies her ass while purring "One owner, low mileage, clean." Adding chauvinistic insult to injury, Morris tells her "You got a shape that'll sell tickets, I'll guarantee you parts and labor on that."

FUN FACT: The venue featured for the derby bouts is the Olympic Auditorium at Eighteenth and Grand in Los Angeles. Now a Korean church, the Olympic was built in 1924 as a sports venue and was home to many real-life derby events (some of the scenes from *Rocky* were filmed here, too).

DOWN AND DERBY

FANTASY ISLAND: "THE WAR GAMES/QUEEN OF THE BOSTON BRUISERS" (1978)
Season 2, Episode 6
DIRECTOR: Earl Bellamy
STORY: Frank Dandridge
CAST: Ricardo Montalban, Herve Villechaize, Anne Francis, Mary Jo Catlett

PLOT SYNOPSIS: Drusilla "Rowdy" Roberts (Francis) goes to Fantasy Island with the dream of becoming a refined lady for the week. Rowdy believes she needs to hide her rough-and-tumble profession from the family of her daughter's fiancé—the high falutin' Wendovers. Under the careful tutelage of Mr. Roarke and Tattoo, she learns the basics of etiquette and the names of some artists (for some reason she's quizzed on the Panama Canal as well; unclear why that's important). But the night before the wedding, she's outed by her derby rival—Hooligan Hanreddy. Looks like the wedding is all but done for when Mr. Roarke jumps in with a dramatic speech that saves the day.

BEST DERBY MOMENT: Tattoo watches some footage of Rowdy and Hooligan brawling with each other on the track. There's a fun header over the railing and some silly half-time shenanigans highlighting the rivalries that played such a big role in derby during the sixties and seventies.

WORST DERBY MOMENT: In the big climactic scene, Rowdy rolls her enemy onto a buffet table. After sliding Hooligan through what appears to be several different pupu platters, she dunks her head in a giant punch bowl. We know old-school derby was staged, but honestly, you'll find better choreography at a kindergarten Easter pageant.

FUN FACTS: This is just one of two derby-themed Fantasy Island episodes. In 1982, there was another episode called "Roller Derby Dolls/Thanks a Million" featuring Vic Tayback (better known as the chef Mel on the TV show *Alice*). He played the manager of a sporting goods store who wanted to own the Brownsville Belles derby team.

KING OF THE HILL: "ARLEN CITY BOMBER" (2005)
Season 9, Episode 10
DIRECTOR: Kyounghee Lim
WRITER: Jonathan Collier
CAST: Kathy Najimy, Brittany Murphy, Mike Judge, Dave Thomas

PLOT SYNOPSIS: Luanne is deep in credit card debt, so she's forced to take on a second job. As a skater with Arlen's roller derby team, she's promised she'll make $500 a game. Once her Aunt Peggy gets a taste of the sport, she signs on, too. But when their first checks arrive, they are for a mere $90. Turns out the team owner makes deductions for everything from water to bandages.

Peggy decides it's time for the skaters to ditch their sleazy manager and become skater owned and operated. They each invest $1,000 of their own money, but democracy proves a challenge for the team. Soon they're fighting with each other and the team breaks up . . . until Peggy hatches the perfect plan to recoup their losses.

BEST DERBY MOMENT: Luanne and Peggy, under their new derby guises of Gold Dust and the Executionator, practice skating around the driveway. Peggy's husband Hank asks why she's doing derby—if it's for the cash or because she just wants to smash into people. Peggy gives a long explanation about how her derby career will provide her with the cash to buy new patio furniture for the family. And as she skates away, she mutters under her breath "and I like to smash into people!"

WORST DERBY MOMENT: When the team holds its first practice, infighting quickly ensues as pivots, blockers, and jammers argue about whose job is most important. For any skater that has lived through real-life derby drama—this part hits a little too close to home.

DOWN AND DERBY

FUN FACT: To research this episode, "King of the Hill" creator Mike Judge and several of the show's writers went to a Texas Roller-girls game in Austin.

CSI: NY: "JAMALOT" (2005)
Season 2, Episode 210
DIRECTOR: Jonathan Glassner
WRITER: Andrew Lipsitz
CAST: Gary Sinise, Melina Kanakaredes, Cameron Goodman, Shanti Wintergate, Noa Tishby

PLOT SYNOPSIS: The roller derby plot line of this episode revolves around a banked track team called the Manhattan Minx, gals who look more like waitresses from Hooters than genuine derby girls. The Minx's rising star is a pretty girl with the ridiculous and XFL inspired name She Hate Me. She Hate Me dies during a bout following an infield melee. Turns out it wasn't the cat fighting that did her in, but rather massive organ failure due to hypothermia. Careful investigation reveals that someone was putting a weight loss drug in the skater's shampoo!

In true *CSI* fashion, the detectives go through a list of possible suspects—the team's coach, rival skaters, the misfit rookie. We won't reveal the killer, but let's just say . . . getting into derby solely for financial profit is never a good idea. Crime doesn't pay (and derby rarely does either!).

BEST DERBY MOMENT: Ummmm . . . The skating is a far cry from an honest portrayal of modern day derby. There is one fun forensic moment where you see what the effect of a skate wheel rolling through a pool of blood would be. Beyond that, there's not a lot to recommend here, except seeing L.A. Derby Doll Tara Armov (known for wearing nothing but black) in a neon green boutfit.

WORST DERBY MOMENT: The scene where the Manhattan Minx skaters are in the locker room clad in nothing but their Victoria's Secret best and a ridiculous amount of make-up. Their smarmy manager weighs them and shakes his head disapprovingly at skaters who have the tiniest bit of extra meat on their bones. As retired TXRD Lonestar Rollergirl Lux remarked, "Could you imagine all of us standing around in our bra and panties happily waiting around to get the stamp of approval from our male leader? *Ha*!"

FUN FACT: The bout footage at the opening features a number of present and former L.A. Derby Dolls, including Tara Armov, Red Jenn, Molly Hatchett, Dita Slayworth, and Frida Fondle. Tara says the actress playing Polly Part'em, Noa Tishby, was very eager to learn about derby. She started blocking around with Tara who instinctively knocked Tishby on her ass. Tara says the crew wouldn't let Tishby anywhere near her after that. "Don't hit the actresses," they kept admonishing the derby girls on set, "They'll bruise!"

PSYCH: "TALK DERBY TO ME" (2008)
Season 3, Episode 7
DIRECTOR: Steve Miner
WRITER: Tim Meltreger
CAST: James Roday, Dulé Hill, Maggie Lawson, Mickie James, Sydney Bennett

PLOT SYNOPSIS: At the scene of a department store burglary, detective Shawn Spencer notices a mark on the floor left by a skate wheel. He suspects the thieves must be members of the local flat-track roller derby team, so he suggests fellow investigator Juliet O'Hara go undercover. Juliet signs on as a skater named "Maniac" and soon discovers that some of the skaters have, in fact, been up to no good. Once fellow skaters discover that Maniac is onto them, they try to permanently silence her.

BEST DERBY MOMENT: When Shawn realizes that the criminal rollergirls are about to take down Juliet, he starts to panic. His partner Gus steps up to the plate by quickly donning a pair of skates and hopping on the track. As Blondie's "One Way or Another" plays, he

DOWN AND DERBY

slams into a skater named Speed Freak and sends her flying into the crowd. Grinning with pride, he wheels around just in time to see two other skaters who proceed to tackle him to the ground.

WORST DERBY MOMENT: During a jam, team captain Kamikaze takes the time to reach down to her skate, pull off a piece of duct tape and daintily place it on the back of one of her opponents. This move is supposed to indicate to another teammate that the marked skater should be knocked down. But this is roller derby, not hanging art at a gallery! Seriously, during a bout, who has the time or inclination to do something like that? You want someone to go down, just do it!

FUN FACT: One of the skaters, Rita "Lethal Weapon" Westwood, was played by Mickie James, a professional wrestler who's earned the title of WWE Divas Champion.

Also filling out the cast were many members of the Terminal City Rollergirls of Vancouver, Canada. Among them was Cinder Hella, whose big moment came in a scene where she is knocked out-of-bounds and goes flying onto the floor. Cinder Hella notes that she performed the stunt without any extra padding. "It felt like we did about twenty takes, but I lost track," she recalls. "My souvenir was a really pretty, hand-sized bruise from the repetitive falls on my hip, but this was nothing next to banging my tailbone in a half-pipe mishap months before."

KATH & KIM: "COMPETITION" (2009)
Season 3, Episode 7
DIRECTOR: Randall Einhorn
WRITER: Jim Dubensky
CAST: Molly Shannon, Selma Blair, John Michael Higgins, Ron White, L.A. Derby Dolls

PLOT SYNOPSIS: In order to get hitched to her honey, Phil, Kath Day must first get divorce papers signed by her ex-hubby, Rusty Day, owner of a banked-track derby league. Kath visits Rusty's Roller Derby warehouse (a.k.a. the L.A. Derby Doll Factory) to get his John Hancock just as one of his star skaters quits. Rusty makes a deal with Kath—he'll sign, but only if she lets her daughter, Kim, skate for his team.

Kim is stoked about the idea, despite her mom's warnings about the rigors of the sport. Kim, who takes on the derby name Justine Timberskate, starts practicing with the team (played by Dolls such as Ryder Hard, Stiv Skator, and Janis Choplin) and has a blast with them.

But, come her first game, Justine finds out how violent derby can get. Just as her derby career swiftly comes to an end, her momma, Kath, saves the day on the track. As Destruction Day, Kath jams full of vengeance (and in an outfit that looks like a satiny reject from *Unholy Rollers*).

BEST DERBY MOMENT: Before Kim's big debut, Kath gives her a pair of Pepto-Bismol pink bedazzled elbow pads—the same ones she used to use back in the day. It's a sweet moment of mother-daughter derby bonding until Kim asks "What's that smell?" Mom replies, "That's the smell of victory, twenty-five-year-old sweat and Jean Nate After-Bath Splash!"

WORST DERBY MOMENT: As a jammer, Justine gets rammed vagina-first into the railing. She flies over the track and crashes into a table below, before falling to the floor. Even if it's a television show and not real derby, it's still hard to watch without shuddering.

Also painful is watching girls we know and adore in real life playing skaters on a team owned by a drunk, callous fat dude with roots in dire need of a dye job. And seriously, you have a badass derby team and the best you could do is call them "Rusty's Roller Derby Team"?

FUN FACT: Being on a TV show is a lot of fun . . . Filming a TV show is sometimes a bit less exciting, as the Derby Dolls on this shoot learned firsthand. There were many hours of waiting around and not doing much at all. Tawdry Tempest, always one to stir things up, started engaging skaters in a round of what she calls "sexy stretching" to keep everybody entertained. "I kept waiting for the director to tell us to stop or tone it down," she recalls, "but they never did."

PROFILE: Krissy Krash And Iron Maiven

MARC "STALKERAZZI" CAMPOS

In the ensemble of players that make up the L.A. Derby Dolls' Tough Cookies, fiery captain Iron Maiven, and fearsome blocker Krissy Krash are two characters that keep the crowd on their feet—and opponents off theirs. The role of real-life roller derby all-stars is one that they inhabit with seasoned gusto, but when they were cast as the Manson Sisters in the film *Whip It!*, the teammates found themselves in unfamiliar territory—creating derby on demand.

Q: How did you two get the roles on Whip It!?

IRON MAIVEN: I asked myself that same question a few times! Drew Barrymore and friends started showing up to our bouts early in the season. Next thing I know, I get an e-mail from our league founder saying we've been invited to an audition to read lines. Sure, talk about awkward.

DOWN AND DERBY

Here, um, let me put you in a room, in front of a camera and Drew Barrymore. Now act, act like you've never acted before! Oh that's right, I have never acted before.

KRISSY KRASH: First time Drew came to a game, I went up to say "hi" because my stepmom wanted me to take a picture. Drew was like, "Oh, Braids, nice game out there!" She was nice enough, so I asked her if she was having fun, did she enjoy derby, blah, blah, blah. She's like, "Ummm, yeah . . . I'm making a movie about it."

IM: I'd say like a week later, the all-star teams were asked to participate in a skating audition—fun! Krissy and I both had callbacks but had no idea what we were auditioning for or what character we might be acting like. We sorta cornered Drew and were ever so slyly trying to pry some info out of her—like "so should we be brushing up on those lines you gave us last audition?" And she got all excited and wide-eyed and said, "No, you ladies are going to try out for the Manson sisters!" (like seriously, so excited, as if we had any idea what she was talking about). She continues, "You know, you're kinda like the Hanson brothers from *Slap Shot*, but you're deaf!" Krissy and I just looked at each other. As if acting without ever acting before was hard enough, now we have to pretend like we can't hear anything?!

KK: We are both freaking-out excited. We show up and they explain that they want us to act out some scenes without using any words. We pretend to be drunk and fake sign stuff to each other about boys, and we do a scene where we ruin the game.

IM: The audition was so scary! One of the scariest moments in my life; scary like I don't know what to do scary. Drew and Barry, the producer, kept having us repeat things over and over and kept making faces like they just popped a bunch of Sour Patch Kids in their mouths. "Eeeeee, I don't know", they kept saying. Krissy and I walked out with an "aw, what the heck, we gave it our best shot" attitude and then said, "See you at practice."

Q: *What was the most challenging thing about skating in a movie versus skating in a real bout?*

KK: Movie skating is much slower than derby skating. We spent a lot of time choreographing the action scenes. In real derby, I can let my body act instinctively to what's going on in the pack. In movie derby, you have to follow the plan, no matter how much you want to clobber the jammer. On the plus side, no one at the game will bring me a green tea in between jams. Movie derby had its perks.

IM: My entire derby career, I've assured people our roller derby isn't staged. And now, here I am, staging roller derby for a movie. That is really hard to do! You don't even make it around the track once! The amount of space that actually appears on screen at once is no more than ten feet or less of track. And whatever action we were trying to perform, whether it be hits, or even just skating, those actions had to be spot on, on cue, on the mark, or you had to do it all over again! Oh! And not actually hitting people, but making it look like you were.

Q: How much sign language did you have to learn for your roles?

IM: The movie hired a local translator who worked mostly in hospitals translating for the deaf. We didn't know where to start. We had been given a few books that we started looking at, trying to find the language for things like "sister" and "hit," but shockingly there was no roller derby verbiage in these books! Sisters, our coach said, would start to take on a language of their own, using one signal or two mushed together signals to get the point across. We created all sorts of derby terms—jammer, through the pack, rotating—and were able to use existing terms to define "us, wall, up front." We were never exactly sure what Drew wanted from our characters, so we played around with all sorts emotions attached to whatever scenes we were working on. When we started filming we found Drew was really interested in that deadpan expression, sorta, "I don't care that you're talking to me and I can't hear you. I'm here to skate and be tough."

KK: I am not sure who got more of a kick out of us—us or our instructor—but we were all cracking up unstoppably during our lessons. Maiv and I would get super-goofy and end up saying things like "hit the laundry" instead of "take her out." There was only one scripted sign line in the movie. I drunkenly confessed my love for our coach, Razor, but it was cut out, which was probably for the best, since I may have ended up saying something about squirrel vodka instead. Mostly, we ended up using thumbs up and the sign for beer a lot.

Q: What was your favorite memory of working on the film?

KK: Derby summer camp! It was a dream come true. The first two weeks we were there, we showed up to the warehouse around seven AM for yoga, then a few hours of skating, then off to sign language lessons, then more skating. I couldn't believe I was getting paid to do that! All the real derby skaters and actresses skated together. We really bonded. By the time we were ready to shoot, it was like we were a real derby team.

IM: This one night, right before we began actual shooting, we all went out to a local bar for karaoke. At first, it was just a small handful of us singing—Krissy, Kasey Bomber, Eve, Skate Outta Compton (Atlanta Rollergirls), Sacralicious (Lonestar Rollergirls), and Juliette Lewis. Then later the place got packed. Well, there was a box of props on the stage. And in the bottom of that box was a miniature tambourine—like the size of my hand. Next thing I know, not only do I think I am an amazing karaoke singer, but I am also playing back-up tambourine for every single person that stepped foot on that stage. And you better believe I didn't let any singer feel left out by not gracing them with my stage presence and killer tambourine skills. I played that thing for four hours straight. I was slapping it on my thigh so hard, for so long that I gave myself a bruise the exact size of that tambourine, about a good four inches in diameter. And guess what? In movies, there is a little thing called continuity. Manson Sister #1 can't have a bruise on her leg in scene #1 at the track, but have that bruise be gone later in scene #2 at the bar. Oh, my poor makeup lady covered up that bruise everyday until it was gone.

Derby bruises, yeah. I suffer my worst at the after-parties.

Q: What was your favorite skating scene in the movie?

KK: I love the scene where Razor pays the other coach to do his plays because we are all blowing him off and not taking him seriously. The opposing team uses our play and totally takes us out. It was a fun scene to film, and it turned out great.

IM: As much as I just griped over doing staged roller derby, it was really fun to stage things that looked really good, but most likely would never happen in real derby. Like that scene Krissy described. The entire other team manages to block us all out with a good solid stop block. Four skaters timing it out and turning all at the same time to knock down four skaters. That was kinda fun.

Q: Did working together on Whip It! make you stronger teammates in real life?

IM: Krissy and I were together all the time. Our rooms were next to each other, we shared a trailer, we had the same call times . . . and we got along very well, so it made us closer as friends, which in turn strengthened our trust and teamwork on the track. We're very comfortable around each other and able to be open, communicate our thoughts, and work together well.

KK: We spent a lot of time together and really got to know each other. I couldn't have asked for a better person to play my sister. By the end of the whole thing, we could practically read each other's minds. We still use the sign language we learned on the track. It's actually pretty helpful!

ACKNOWLEDGEMENTS

LIKE THE SPORT of derby itself, this book has really been a collective effort by all the skaters, support staff, and derby fans who have contributed their time, anecdotes, and encouragement. For all the gals and guys that have kicked our asses on the track and at the after-parties over the years, we thank you for not letting up when it came to kicking our asses into writing this book.

Likewise, we would like to thank our fantastic editorial pack—Denise Oswald, Anne Horowitz, and Soft Skull Press for their stellar assists through all the literary blockers. Thanks to Ted Weinstein, our terrific agent and Team *Down and Derby*'s star jammer, without whom we never would have scored. Much appreciation to designer Pauline Neuwirth for making us look so good at the end of the game.

Big sweaty hugs to all our hilarious and talented guest authors—Dolly Rocket, Helen Fury, Miss Moxxxie, and Roxy Rockett.

We would also like to thank the following for their invaluable contributions to the artwork: Jay Vollmar (for creating the prettiest cover girl ever); Jenny Comperda (for her generous design assistance); all of our amazingly kind photo contributors—especially Joe Schwartz, Jules Doyle, Mark "Stalkerazzi" Campos, Paul Robertson, Boss Hogg, Darren Michaels, Craig Lammes, Beth Been, Penny Smith, Michael Coyote, Kerry McLain, and Gary

Powers of the Roller Derby Hall of Fame for access to all of your invaluable archives.

To some of our derby crushes, and favorite skaters, we thank you for allowing us to get personal and feature you in our profiles: Kamikaze Kim, Jackie Daniels (Team Haggard unite!), Quadzilla, Queen Elizabitch, Iron Maiven, Ellen "Hurt Vonnegut" Page, Krissy Krash, Polly Purgatory, the incomparable Hydra, Luce Bandit, the legendary Cherry Chainsaw, the soon to be legendary Spawna Chainsaw, Tequila Mockingbird, Justice Feelgood Marshall, Randy Pan, Ms. D'Fiant, Ivanna S. Pankin, Trish the Dish, and our lovely gear model, Mötley Crüz.

Extra special thanks the captain of Team *Whip It!*, Drew Barrymore, for the great opportunity to call you boss for a few months. Ellen, Zoë, Eve, Kristin, Ari, Alia, Jimmy, Andrew, Landon, and Juliette—we salute you. Thanks to Mandate Pictures and Flower Films (Chris Miller, you rock!). We are incredibly grateful for the wonderful ladies at Fox Searchlight, especially Sonia Freeman and Samantha Bond, for all your help and support. A particularly big "hell yes!" goes to our favorite New Yorker from Los Angeles, Karen Neasi.

For La Muerta, Sparkle, Chassis, Celia, Chola, Thora, Demolicious, Val Capone, Smarty Pants, and all the derby legends—our lives have been changed for the better by you all. Your continued support and friendship is what has kept us inspired and rolling forward.

To our readers and expert panel, Val Capone, Hambone, Jeff Miller, Kim Lisagor, and Shauna Cross: We are lucky to have you.

We'd be nowhere without our Netflix queues filled with truly awful movies, dreams of the Mexican Riviera, the editing skills of Emily Richards, the House of Pies, and the thirty-seven Yahoo Groups we are very eager to ignore for a while. To our beloved Salty Sailors—you know who you are—*hot yam!*

Additionally, Kasey would like to thank Timurphy (for all the tequila), Kent Hagen, my "coworkers" Roxie and Niko (and their mom for loaning me their services), Mark Schwind, Mike Legat, Heidi Kraus, Brad Cook, and Jeff Miller once again for all the support he's given me always. To Megan Graham: I'm so fortunate